BUILT
ON
PURPOSE

LESSONS IN LEADERSHIP AND CULTURE

PAUL PETERA

To Andrea and Abby,
for being the reason why

CONTENTS

Introduction:

Built on Purpose

Technology has evolved at a staggering pace. Leadership, however, has not kept up.

Consider this: more than 150 million Americans now carry iPhones with more computing power than all of NASA's systems combined in 1969, the year we landed on the moon. When I graduated from college in 1991, stock trades took five days to settle (it's one day now). Email wasn't common, and we processed transactions on green-screen terminals using instructions from dot matrix printouts. Research meant a day-long trip to the library that might have included microfiche. Today, artificial intelligence can do hours of research work in seconds.

Over the past three-plus decades, as the world has transformed, our collective leadership capabilities have felt stagnant. Despite all the tools at our fingertips, guiding and influencing others towards a common goal and purpose remains one of our greatest challenges.

Well-managed, enduring organizations don't exist without strong leadership. That's hardly a controversial idea, yet there are poorly led organizations everywhere. One could argue that our collective leadership capabilities have not kept pace with the exponential progress we've made in other areas, and it's having crippling effects on productivity, progress and personal growth.

So how do we fix that? One leader at a time, starting with ourselves.

Improving as a leader became a personal priority for me, especially in the latter half of my career. I saw firsthand the difference strong leadership made, not just for the organizations I worked with, but more importantly, for the people I served. If you're reading this, I hope it matters to you, too.

Early in my career, I believed good leadership was about decisiveness, competence, and execution. But after decades of wins, missteps, and reflection, I've learned that the most effective leaders operate from a place of self-awareness and purpose. They see the systems they're part of. They see themselves. And they see how the two constantly influence each other. The best leaders understand the long-term impact they can have and step intentionally into that responsibility.

This is a book about that journey.

It's not a "how-to" manual filled with checklists, and you won't find foolproof blueprints or formulas; true leadership doesn't work that way. Instead, you'll find questions that matter. You'll encounter stories, some from my own journey and others from leaders I've been fortunate enough to walk alongside. I hope they stay with you. And you'll see frameworks built not on theory, but on lived experience.

This book is for the leader who wants to do more than deliver results. It's for the leader who wants to create trust, build culture, and leave people and organizations better than they found them. If you've ever found yourself wondering how to improve alignment on a team, clarify purpose, navigate change, influence others or find the right structure for real impact, I believe you'll find something here.

Over my 30-plus year career, I've worked directly for around 20 bosses and interacted with hundreds of leaders. I've watched. I've taken notes. I've learned.

I wrote this book to share the lessons I've gathered, to pay it forward. These lessons come from victories, and perhaps more importantly, from losses. I don't pretend to have it all figured out, and I don't consider myself an expert. But I am a lifelong learner. We'll never have all of the answers, and that's exactly the point. We're all on our own journey, and if we're doing it right, we're learning a little more each day. Getting better, slowly but surely, with humility.

Each chapter will conclude with **Reflection Prompts** and **Intentional Actions**. The prompts are questions designed to help you to explore your own leadership through the chapter's lens. You might journal your responses, discuss them with a mentor or team, or simply sit with them quietly. The actions offer ways to apply that insight into your daily work. Because while self-awareness is where leadership begins, growth truly happens when insight meets practice.

We'll talk about trust; not as a buzzword, but as the core ingredient of every strong culture.

We'll explore strategy; not as a document, but as a mindset rooted in clarity.

We'll revisit culture; not as a written-and-forgotten mission statement, but as the sum of your daily behavior and the behaviors of those who follow you.

Most of all, we'll reflect on how to lead, not perfectly, but intentionally. With honesty. With curiosity. With purpose. This is how we accelerate our leadership capabilities and pay it forward to those who follow in our footsteps. Then perhaps we can marvel at how far we've come in leadership.

Because in the end, how we elevate ourselves and those around us isn't just meaningful; it may be the most important thing we do.

PART I: THE INNER WORK

Leadership That Starts with Purpose

Chapter 1:

People Are Always Watching

Steve Beck was an affable, hard-working family man who led a margin operations team at a regional brokerage firm in Richmond, VA. He was my first manager in financial services, twelve years my senior, and hailed from the small town outside of Richmond where I was raised. Steve's team was filled with similarly affable and hard-working young professionals. People liked working for and with Steve, who greeted everyone with an easy-going "Hey there!" spoken in a slight southern drawl. Everyone on the team was comfortable around Steve, who was capable of giving as well as taking a ribbing that never escalated beyond good-natured.

I had been fascinated with financial services since I was a kid, so I took to this firm and Steve's team as a sponge takes to water. I still smile at the vivid memories from this part of my career. I worked hard, I learned and I laughed. Every single day. I wasn't making any money, and it really didn't matter.

Though I was learning daily how to do my job, what hadn't yet clicked for me was that learning the tasks of the job was just the beginning. I had earned a couple of quick promotions based on my mastery of the subject matter and my work ethic, but I was laughably green and not yet ready to make a difference.

Part of the reason for this was that I didn't yet understand how my job fit into the bigger picture, which was not uncommon for young professionals still finding their way. I hadn't figured out systematically how our department was impacted by what happened in other departments, and vice versa. I didn't fully appreciate the impact our role had on the client and financial advisor. And what were the risk and regulatory implications of what we did? I still had a lot to learn.

But there was something else I was missing. It was more nuanced, less black and white, and something you didn't read in department procedures: interpersonal dynamics, influence, organizational culture. And the gateway to all of it: self-awareness.

Seeing potential in me, Steve called me into his office one afternoon. I was at ease in Steve's office because, in addition to respecting his knowledge, I genuinely trusted that he wanted me to get the most out of my time there. Getting the point quickly, he said, "Paul, I want you to remember that people are *always* watching you. Even when you think they aren't."

His advice was rooted in an attempt to help me improve my emotional intelligence and, in particular, self-awareness. Steve understood that people watch their leaders closely. They take cues from how leaders respond, verbally and non-verbally, to the events around them. They see how leaders praise and how they criticize. How they plan and follow-through. How they celebrate victory and absorb defeat.

You can learn a lot by observing the behavior of other leaders. Many of my own behaviors have been shaped from watching others over the years - both good and bad! Believe me, I kept a list. This started early, and as I grew, it influenced how I tried to approach leadership.

It proved hugely helpful.

Whatever your preferred method, I'd highly recommend tracking your observations. Take the time to understand how leaders interact with people up and down the organization, their temperament, their thoughtfulness, how they handle pressure and success, their authenticity. Watch how these traits impact others' behaviors, attitudes and engagement.

Steve viewed me as an emerging leader, even at my young age, and knew that self-awareness was not yet a strength of mine. If I didn't make progress in this area, it could negatively impact our small group in the near term, and I would struggle to develop as a leader over time.

The advice was important, and Steve was incredibly kind to share it with me. Looking back, it was much deeper and more reciprocal than I realized – which makes sense. If I had been watching others' behavior in a never-ending pursuit of better leadership traits, *of course* other people are watching me in their pursuit of theirs. And even when they weren't doing so intentionally, their behavior and approach to their job would still be impacted by my behavior. This is grassroots culture at its core.

It is a huge responsibility on us as leaders to fully understand this. I would be remiss if I didn't stress that we all have a leadership responsibility, regardless of our professional role or title.

IT ALL STARTS WITH SELF-AWARENESS

Everything in this book is more relevant when you start with self-awareness. Put another way, without it, you won't grow and the organizations you lead won't thrive.

We all carry a kind of energy as leaders. Some leaders walk into a room and instantly shift the mood, for better or worse. Others move more subtly, with their presence leaving ripples in conversations long after they've left.

When we are self-aware - understanding how we respond to people, problems, opportunities, disappointment, victories - we are sure to become more successful leaders. We will appreciate how our words and actions impact others' behavior and the success or our teams. And that will unlock our ability to be more intentional about our behavior, tone, word choice, timing – all of it.

The question I started asking myself was a simple one: *What kind of ripple, if any, am I leaving?*

I came to understand over time that this ripple was more impactful than I had given it credit for. I also discovered that the ripple I was leaving wasn't always intentional on my part, especially the more subtle the behaviors or actions were.

Self-awareness requires us to be in the moment, to read the room. It also requires us to reflect *after* the moment on what felt "right" and "not quite right" and diagnose it; not to be harsh on ourselves but to give ourselves permission to learn and improve. So, I started jotting notes after key meetings or speeches about how I thought they went, and what were my "did wells" and "next times."

But as the old saying goes, "You can't read the label from inside the jar." Eventually I invited trusted colleagues to tell me how *they* thought the meetings or speeches went to see if there were discrepancies and to help me see myself clearly. That's when I discovered that self-awareness is both a solo pursuit and a team sport. Over time, there were fewer discrepancies or surprises, but never zero. After all, we are human and interpersonal dynamics are, well, dynamic. The learning never stops!

Objectively, these are data points. Not all feedback will be valuable; however, the more you seek it out, the better you get at discerning what is helpful. And when you have trusted relationships built with those from whom you're seeking feedback, you will be more willing to digest next-level suggestions all in the name of self-improvement.

It's not too dissimilar to the agile methodology in project management that favors flexibility, collaboration and iterative development. It's okay to fail, but fail fast. If the feedback you hear, or your own growing awareness, tells you that something didn't work, remember it, change course and move on. You might even have a sense of humor about it, but above all else don't dwell on it.

A byproduct of self-awareness-driven behavior is that the people who are watching will see that you recognize you're not perfect and also that you're an active participant in your personal growth. Both are endearing qualities that may lead to an even stronger followership. Plus, those you've invited to share their perspective will be more apt to be torch-bearers for you and the culture you're building.

However, most of us have a long way to go.

Tasha Eurich is an organizational psychologist. In her book *Insight*, Ms. Eurich said that while 95% of people believe they are self-aware, only 10-15% actually are. To help us improve, she agreed that self-reflection and seeking out honest feedback are important. Her research also said that we often do this incorrectly. Ms. Eurich said we sabotage our own effort in introspection by asking ourselves the right question the wrong way.

We often ask "Why" something happened, which doesn't lead us towards the truth, but away from it. Instead of asking ourselves, "Why do I feel terrible?" we should ask "What situations make me feel terrible and what do they have in common?" Instead of, "Why was that meeting such a disaster?" we should ask, "What about the meeting agenda, attendees and interactions made it unsuccessful?"

Asking "what" allows us to more objectively discern what can be corrected, and lowers the chance that our brains will trap us in a cycle of negative thoughts and emotions. Give that a try next time you do a "post-mortem".

WHAT HUMILITY TEACHES US

Perhaps more importantly, self-awareness means having the ability to understand our own thoughts, feelings and behaviors. It means knowing and accepting our strengths and weaknesses, which helps unlock humility as a leadership trait.

I was fortunate to recently strike up a friendship with Dutch Baughman. I first knew of Dutch as the athletic director at Virginia Tech who hired the legendary Frank Beamer as football coach back in 1986. I came to learn that Baughman's illustrious career was a leadership journey shaped by personal influences, from Hall of Fame coach Woody Hayes at Ohio State to a who's who of leadership thinkers like Steven Covey, John Maxwell and Jim Collins. His journey included founding the Lead1 Association's annual institute, a three-day forum that prepares senior level athletic administrators to become athletic directors.

If anyone simultaneously embodies both a larger-than-life and down-to-earth persona, it is Dutch Baughman. He has walked with, learned from and positively impacted some of the country's most prominent minds. Yet he'll make you feel as if you've been sitting on the porch talking with him your entire life.

When I got the opportunity to spend some time with Dutch, a man whose leadership legacy spans five decades, I listened closely. I wanted to know how a seasoned leader reflects on a lifetime of impact. His stories reinforced what I've come to believe deeply: humility is a leader's greatest strength.

I want to share two anecdotes that Baughman shared with me regarding humility. The first was a story from his time as a graduate assistant coach under Coach Hayes. Baughman had previously played for Hayes, who had subsequently called him back to Columbus, Ohio to join his staff.

Meeting with him the first day, Hayes slid a hard bound book across the desk. As he did so, Hayes instructed that if Baughman read this book that he was about to give him, he'd be right up to speed with the rest of the staff. The title of the book was *What I Know About Football* by W.W. Hayes."

Baughman recalled, "We finished the meeting, and I get out in the hallway. I couldn't wait to see what was in this book. I open the book, and every page is blank. I turned to go back in and to tell coach I think I got the bad one in the box. There are no words in this book. He looked at me and said, 'You're going to be amazed at what you're going to learn from a book that has no words in it.' And so, from that day until today, that book sits on the corner of my desk right next to my Bible. I figure one book has got all the words, and one's got none. And I learned from both of them."

The great Woody Hayes, a Hall of Fame coach with multiple national championships, was illustrating humility by instilling in his young coach that learning, listening and observation are leadership multipliers, and that even Hayes didn't know it all.

The second story came from Baughman's longtime interactions with Jim Collins. It was Collins' book *Good to Great*, of course, which posited that leaders who blend personal humility with intense professional will are the most effective. Baughman shared with me the discussions he had with Collins about how he reached this conclusion.

Over countless interviews with Fortune 500 leaders, Collins and his staff tried to find a common thread about enduring leaders, those that lasted the longest and were highly respected. They found that what was apparent in every one was something that wasn't specifically asked about. That something was humility.

Baughman said, "What they discovered was the *Level 5* leader (considered most effective) is the one that has the highest level of integrity and humility for their professional and their personal decisions. They're all humble. If there's something that goes wrong, it's their fault. When something goes right, it's everybody else who gets the praise."

It was refreshing to see the level of importance Baughman places on the responsibility of leadership. I wish we saw it in more people. The numerous stories he shared with me about humility in leadership was also extremely validating, as it's been a priority of mine for quite a while.

Humility is a liberating thing. The great poet Nikki Giovanni said, "Once you know you are, you don't have to worry anymore." This insight captures the heart of humility. Once you freely accept that you don't know everything and you never will, your reward is the freedom of becoming a lifelong learner.

This freedom unlocks the ability to learn from experiences over time - what worked and what didn't work. How handling a situation a certain way impacted others in ways both good and bad. To me, experience is the greatest education because it's tangible and pertinent and personal to you. Experiences accumulate and compound like an investment portfolio over the decades. And you find yourself calling upon experiences from the past, sometimes seemingly unrelated, that help you through the problems of today. Twenty-five-year-old me would not have comprehended that.

Having humility also lowers defensiveness, which allows you to accept coaching or ask others to educate you. It unlocks so much of your ability to learn across the spectrum. There is a certain feeling of liberation that comes from saying, "I don't know the first thing about that. Share with me what *you* know!"

CREATING A CULTURE OF AUTHENTICITY

Finally, humility frees you up to build a team around you filled with people that excel at the things that you do not. In my career, I have built a tool chest filled with an array of experiences, though I've seldom been the foremost expert about the subject matter related to my jobs. There will always be someone out there that knows more than I do. Knowing this, I prefer hiring people who could run circles around me regarding a particular subject or skill.

For instance, I have a good feel for organizational constructs and interpersonal dynamics, but I'm also a horrible salesperson. Therefore, I always make sure there are people on my team that can think and operate like salespeople.

And despite decades of broad experience in operational risk management, my depth of fraud expertise specifically, relevant to today's financial services ecosystem will never be best-in-class. It can't be because I don't spend all of my time there. I am much better off handing that responsibility to a fraud expert ("What do *you* think we should do here?").

Logistically, it's next to impossible to be an expert at every facet of operational risk. Worse, if I were to purport to be an expert at every facet, others would see right through that, I'd lose credibility, and our performance and culture would suffer as a result.

As Simon Sinek has said, "the role of a leader is not to come up with all the great ideas. It's to create an environment in which great ideas can happen."

Knowing your limitations is part of what helps you to become an authentic leader, which is crucial if you want a strong team filled with talented people who want to follow you. Empower these people, and they're more likely to believe in your vision, do "extra" for you, and think for themselves.

Self-awareness influences psychological safety, too. If you are unaware of how you come across, that can accidentally create tension or fear on your team, even with the best of intentions. Leaders that appear rushed or dismissive risk squashing creativity or productive discourse on their teams. Giving a team member an official role as the "black hat" in meetings – a license to play devil's advocate – is one intentional way to promote dialogue and debate. Another is directly asking team members for their input. Just know that not everyone is comfortable speaking up in certain settings. In those cases, an early prompt such as, "Tom, we're going to be discussing ways we can improve employee engagement in Thursday's meeting, and I'd love to hear your perspective" can be helpful.

People want to be able to connect with you personally, to know what you're about, and to believe that *you* believe what you're saying.

Intentionality and authenticity are crucial to being a successful leader. I don't believe you can do either very well without first being self-aware. It takes work. Like any muscle, though, it's something you can develop, so prioritizing self-awareness will pay off over time.

While our success may be measured annually by our explicit goals and accomplishments, *how* we succeed and *with whom* we do so is what stays with us long beyond our tenure at a company. In the end, it's relationships and personal impact that define a fulfilling career.

We can learn subject matter from lots of places. Those who made us better leaders and better people are the ones who most often had the biggest impact on us. Our duty is to pay it forward.

HONORING STEVE

Our leadership journey starts with ourselves, with the humble understanding of our responsibility as leaders and the importance of self-awareness as a prerequisite to that journey.

I credit the beginning of my journey to Steve Beck.

He was a good man and a good friend long after our days of working together had ended. I am extremely fortunate to have had him as my first manager. This was partially because the work experience was so positive, but also because the trajectory of self-awareness that he put me on was the first big building block to my growth as a leader.

Steve passed away a few years ago long before he should have, leaving behind a beautiful and loving family and a large number of adoring friends. I revere him as much today as I did when he was still here. I'm thankful that he knew the impact he made on my life, and I've tried very hard to honor him over the years by helping others the way he helped me.

Reflection Prompts

- When was the last time I changed my approach based on feedback?
- What do others admire about my leadership? What do they endure?
- What would my team say it's like to work for me on a stressful day?
- Reflect on a moment when I *thought* I was doing well, then discovered others saw it differently, and vice versa.

Intentional Actions

- Jot down 3–5 reflection questions to ask yourself weekly.
- Keep a journal of your leadership behaviors, and others'.
- Create self-observation prompts to reflect on after meetings.
- Create a feedback circle of trust.

Chapter 2:

What Are You "For"?

Leadership often begins with ambition, whether it be career goals or more responsibility or influence. As you progress in your leadership journey, those outer measures become less fulfilling if they're not matched with inner alignment to your values, purpose or long-term goals – a "true north." Many leaders burn out or stall in their careers due to a lack of clarity about themselves and their own purpose. Similarly, many teams flounder because they lack a true north accompanied by complementary boundaries.

As a leader, it's important to know what you are "for". Being "for" something doesn't just mean having goals, though goals are certainly a part of it. It means having a purpose, embodying values and creating an environment that cultivates them.

Understandably, this requires considerable reflection about what drives you. With that comes questions:

> Am I *for* clarity, or simply *against* confusion?

Am I *for* empowerment, or tired of micromanaging?

Am I *for* doing things the right and honorable way, or *against* being perceived as not?

We don't always take time to answer these questions. In high-performance environments, the reward system is designed to value output, not introspection. Without reflection, however, leadership becomes performative at best; polished outside, unanchored inside.

At worst?

One of the stops on my leadership journey was a promotion to take over a team of professionals in a different part of the company in the early stages of a cost-cutting initiative. It was in an area in which I had familiarity, not expertise. The previous leader had been let go, a move that did not sit well with some on the team I was inheriting. The skepticism in me as the new leader was high and, frankly, justified.

I got to work absorbing as much of the subject matter as I could, and building new relationships across the firm and on the team. I righted some wrongs organizationally and laid groundwork for doing things the right way. Nevertheless, in my time leading that organization, I never truly got beyond trying to execute the already-defined goal. I did not take the time to establish a culture or direction or to fully integrate my beliefs with our goals. I tried to look the part in some respects, which gave reluctant team members further reason not to trust or support my leadership.

The understanding when I took the role was that I would get the team through this transitional phase before moving on. That was the right call, but the temporary nature of the assignment probably exacerbated my weaknesses. As a result, for the entirety of my time in that role, I looked and felt like someone who was keeping the seat warm. In retrospect, I should have seized the opportunity and forged a confident purpose-driven path forward. Perhaps I wasn't ready, but objectively, it wasn't a good fit or good timing.

For several years I considered that short period in my career a failure. The beauty of time, though, is that it gives a person perspective. As it turns out, my experience in this role shaped so much of how I approached every leadership position since then.

Because of that time, I learned to prepare more effectively for every new role, including understanding the ingredients for (and barriers to) success and concurring on what success looks like. I learned to give serious thought to what was important to me and how to articulate that to my team in a way that resonated with them and aligned with our goals. And I learned some valuable lessons about the right way to build and motivate a team.

We all want our career to be a series of successes. In reality, we know that success is never linear. The old saying is that we learn more from our stumbles than our victories. Those learnings have a way of compounding over time. I'm extremely grateful for all of the lessons I've learned, and the circumstances that led to them.

CONNECTION TO ORGANIZATIONAL PURPOSE

It's important for a leader and their team to gain clarity about what the leader is for. But how does a leader's personal clarity assimilate with the team or company? In order to lead to organizational success, that clarity needs to be connected to organizational purpose. It's aligning "what is the leader for?" with "what is the organization for?"

Sure, meeting financial targets is important. Even more important, leaders have to establish a clear and meaningful purpose for the organization. This involves defining an inspiring reason for its existence and uniting leadership around that purpose. When employees at all levels understand how their work supports a greater objective, they feel more motivated and engaged. We will dive deeper into this in Chapter 6.

Many teams flail because no one articulated what "winning" means. Their lack of purpose leads to more firefighting and less meaningful progress. You can spot these teams pretty easily: they work super hard, are often reactive, typically suffer from high turnover and burnout, and regularly lament, "if we only had more headcount…"

Teams and organizations that have a true north are more adept at focusing on the right problems and opportunities. And there's a certain magic of seeing people at every level of the organization state with pride how their job specifically aligns with an organizational goal.

BOUNDARIES ARE A GIFT

Another benefit of an organization with a clear purpose and knowing what it is "for" is that its members are better equipped to say "no" or at least "not yet" when something doesn't align with that purpose.

When a team is aligned on its purpose, it is much easier to define what is "in bounds" and "out of bounds". This can be about prioritization, allowing us to say, "we can't do that right now because it doesn't help us achieve one of our top three goals".

But it could also be about protecting energy, decision-making clarity or cultural true norths. In his book *Essentialism: The Disciplined Pursuit of Less*, Greg McKeon stresses the importance of identifying what is truly essential, then learning to eliminate the non-essential, which means saying no to requests and activities that don't contribute to your core priorities. This leads to fewer distractions, increased focus and, for the team, a feeling of making a more meaningful contribution to what truly matters.

Several years ago, one of my teams had requested an extension on a deliverable due to a significant reorganization and turnover. The team preferred doing the job right over doing it quickly. It was concerned that a rushed effort would reflect poorly on the team as professionals, and increase the risk of future re-work. Due to circumstances out of anyone's control, the team was ultimately bound to the original due date.

Their supervisor told me later, "If you recall, I had written a formal proposal with rationale for an extension past the due date that was accepted, and we proceeded with the new schedule. When the directive came that there was no longer approval for the extension, panic and frustration set in on the team. You came to us immediately and said, 'We will all pitch in, including me, and we'll do our absolute best, but I don't want you to sacrifice doing your work the right way solely to meet a forced timeline.' It truly set the tone and the team appreciated it. I will always be so appreciative of your support in that moment!"

By the way, the team hit their deadline and was justifiably proud. Not just of the result, but how they got there.

This is merely one example of the importance of knowing, communicating and reinforcing the behaviors, actions and norms that are in bounds and out of bounds. When leaders set this standard, alignment improves, culture strengthens and teams execute faster.

AUTHENTICITY IN ACTION

Somewhere along the way, authenticity got conflated with radical transparency, emotional impulsiveness or

disregard for professionalism. We've all heard the
phrases: *"I just tell it like it is,"* or *"That's just who I am."*

But true authenticity isn't about saying or doing whatever
you feel in the moment. It's about aligning
your actions, values, and presence in a way that
is grounded, intentional, and trustworthy (I should clarify
that there are professional boundaries you don't cross. Be
your authentic *business* self.)

It means meaning everything you say.

When you are aligned, you will truly have an opportunity
to earn a followership. When you aren't, there can be
perilous results.

Misalignment often shows up in ways like these:

- A leader who *says* he or she values collaboration
  but consistently shuts down dissenting views
- An executive that *states* innovation is a core value,
  then punishes risk-taking
- A manager who *stresses* the importance of
  "balance" while praising 80-hour weeks

These gaps don't just create confusion. They
create unnecessary friction, both emotional and cultural.
Over time, that friction becomes fatigue.

When people can't reconcile what's being said with what's
being done, they stop listening. They disengage.
Eventually, they leave – or worse, they stay and stop
caring.

In his book *True North*, Bill George defines authentic leadership as staying true to your values and principles, even under pressure. "Authentic leaders are people of the highest integrity, committed to building enduring organizations...They are guided by a deep sense of purpose and the courage to act on it."

That kind of alignment is less about performance than congruence. It's knowing what you stand for, and standing for it even when it's uncomfortable. It takes honest examination, requiring self-awareness, to determine if you are out of alignment.

You don't have to be perfect. None of us are. You just have to want to be better tomorrow than you were today. Progress with integrity. It shows up most clearly when you stop trying to look like a leader and start simply being one.

When it comes to purpose-driven leadership and building a followership, I do not believe in the philosophy of "fake it 'til you make it". That may work as an episodic catalyst to getting out of your comfort zone, but it's not a sustainable leadership method.

There is a certain amount of subject matter expertise that should be considered "table stakes" for the majority of leadership roles. It helps you build business strategy and solve problems, and it gives you credibility. I also believe you don't have to know everything. Far more important is a leader's understanding of organizations, people and purpose combined with the skills to articulate that purpose, provide direction and support the team in becoming high-performing. You can't fake that, and when you do, people know.

Leadership roles of course come with attention. And that attention creates temptation: to sound confident when you're unsure, to say the right things even when your gut says something different, to be polished in a way that fits a certain mold.

Early in my career, I thought good leadership meant knowing more than I should have been expected to know at that time. So, I asked lots of questions and prepared extra hard for meetings; to understand the content, but also to make sure I sounded like I "had it all figured out."

Let's be clear, there's nothing wrong with learning and preparation. However, there were plenty of times in those meetings where I probably chimed in when the best course of action would have been to keep my mouth shut and listen.

There were times when I was not as far along on my emotional intelligence journey where I might assert something because it sounded like what I'd heard leaders assert in the past, but it didn't align with my convictions. It didn't land because it wasn't authentically "me," and it impacted others' behaviors in unintended ways.

A final, somewhat silly, performative example. I am a native of Virginia and have what I consider to be a very slight southern accent. In the first part of my career, lacking in confidence about my knowledge set and more frequently working with Wall Street veterans and New Yorkers, I felt the way I talked might lead others to assume I was less intelligent – certainly not like them – and disregard what I had to say. As a result, I tried to smooth out the way that I talked as if that would make me look more the part. Not a great move.

I didn't realize that trying to look the part actually held me back as a leader because I was leading from image instead of authenticity. Besides, I'm proud of where I'm from!

Eventually, I shed my discomfort about my speaking. In fact, I even managed to employ some of the folksy sayings I grew up with in a way that resonated with my teams. Something they affectionately called "Paul-isms."

Performative leadership is exhausting because it's rooted in external validation rather than internal conviction. You spend more time wondering how you're being perceived than whether you're acting in alignment. It's a waste of energy, it's not productive and it's not effective. After I let go of the absurd notion about the way I talked, I don't ever recall someone dismissing my opinions because of it.

Here are some signs you might be leading performatively:

- You hesitate to speak candidly because it might "disrupt the vibe"
- You overcompensate in areas you feel insecure, instead of seeking help
- You adopt leadership language or behaviors that aren't natural to you

- You focus more on sounding strategic than being strategic

By contrast, purposeful leadership starts with what you're *for* – not who you're trying to impress.

In performative leadership, your attention is on your reputation. In purposeful leadership, your attention is on your values, direction, culture, relationships and impact.

When you lead with purpose, people may not always agree with you. *But they'll know what you're for.* They'll trust your consistency and respect your positions. Over time, more people will follow you because of who you are, not how you look.

That's the kind of leadership that lasts.

Reflection Prompts

- What am I truly *for* as a leader?
- Have I ever led from image rather than alignment, and what did I learn?
- Are my team members clear on what I stand for?
- Where might I be out of alignment between what I say and what I do?
- Have I been avoiding saying or doing something for fear of how it might be received?

Intentional Actions

- Write your own "I am for..." statement.
- Audit your last five leadership decisions – were they driven by purpose or perception?
- Have a clarity conversation with your team – share what you're for and ask members what they think the team is for. Look for alignment gaps.
- Identify one behavior or habit that feels performative, not purposeful.
- Establish your "in bounds/out of bounds" list.

Chapter 3:

The Power of Intentional Leadership

Culture is not found in a policy or a procedure. It's observed and modeled every day through actions, tone, presence, and priorities. It's nurtured, good or bad, by what is reinforced and rewarded, by what is tolerated and what is not.

It's important to note that part of building a culture is setting expectations and managing them consistently. I want professionals on my team that are good at what they do, are easy to do business with, are accountable and follow through on what they say. I won't tolerate unprofessional behavior, poor ethics or excuses.

Going back to the concept of "in bounds and out of bounds" in the previous chapter, if it's important to you, you'll do it, say it, expect it, model it. Consistently and intentionally. Any inconsistency in words versus actions or expectations versus consequences will quickly erode what you've built, culture-wise.

Actions are the evidence of values. And you have all the power in the world to chart your course through your intentions and actions. Over time, your organization's culture is shaped through them.

It starts with your first impressions and with the building and nurturing of relationships. Your culture is solidified in how you show up for your team, from setting the tone to standing up for them and protecting them so team members are free to do their jobs. You need everyone to connect with your vision, so you have to make that connection for them.

INTENTIONAL FIRST IMPRESSIONS

There are literally thousands of quotes about first impressions, which must mean that they're pretty important. Malcom Gladwell has one that resonates with me, from his book *Blink: The Power of Thinking Without Thinking*: "Whenever we have something that we are good at - something we care about - that experience and passion fundamentally change the nature of our first impressions."

There is an understanding that all first impressions are potentially flawed, though Gladwell's quote articulates instances where the impressions may be closer to the mark. First impressions across the board are nevertheless vulnerable to biases and influences, and yet they still matter.

I worked with a gentleman years ago who had a knack for quickly formed decisive opinions about people, and he would share these opinions freely when prompted. It was fascinating to watch. So much so, that I would sometimes bring up names of people in conversation just to hear the Pavlovian response.

(Me): "I met with Kevin Smith today."
(Him): "I wouldn't trust him as far as I could throw him."

(Me): "A compliance issue came up last week, so I looped in Julie Green."
(Him): "She's super smart...she's got a great future."

(Me): "We should invite Bob Jones or John Taylor to our next staff meeting to talk about their current business risks."
(Him): "John Taylor? That guy never shuts up. I swear he just likes to hear himself talk."

I could bring up the same name weeks later, and get the same response, nearly word-for-word. It was as if his brain was involuntarily pulling out a 3x5 index card about the person.

People form opinions about us every day. It could be our subject matter expertise, our leadership style, how we treat others...even our personality quirks or wardrobe choices! Opinions don't have to be accurate to be impactful. They only have to be accurate in others' minds.

For some, it's nearly impossible to change their opinion. The gentleman I worked with may have been an extreme example. Nonetheless, it's true that everyone you connect with has a figurative 3x5 card in their brain about you. Only so much fits on that card, and it's essentially your personal brand. Would you rather have a say on what goes on that card, or leave it to chance?

So, when I had introductory meetings with new colleagues or new employees, I started intentionally practicing active listening to get to know who they were and what was important to them. I'd simply ask them to "tell me your story" and let them go where they wanted, listening intently. I would openly invite their questions and answer just as openly. I'd also make sure they knew they could always call on me if they needed any help, whether to provide context, background or help lower a barrier for them. And of course, a promise such as that requires follow through.

Mostly, I wanted their first impression of me to be that I was interested in them as a person and I valued them.

After seeing an introverted colleague, years earlier, mortified at being recognized publicly in a large gathering, and having the recognition fail in its intended purpose, I started asking new employees how they preferred to receive recognition and feedback. Another question I've always liked to ask people is "if you didn't have any concerns about money, what would you do with your time?" The answers over the years have proven quite revealing about what drove these folks. It allowed me to tailor how I interacted with them, and it sometimes helped me find assignments that would align with their passion. In one instance, when a person so very clearly had a passion far outside of financial services, it even led to encouraging that individual to pursue that passion as a career switch.

The overriding theme here is that you have a tremendous opportunity to put a relationship (and your leadership) on solid footing by being very intentional about creating meaningful first impressions. So, make the effort.

INTENTIONAL RELATIONSHIPS

Leaders who show up consistently, check in on the people in their organizations and networks, and personalize their approach create deeper followership. Building relationships is about creating connectedness, and it takes intentional effort.

A dozen or so years ago, I read a fantastic book by the late former Secretary of State Colin Powell titled *It Worked for Me: In Life and Leadership*. In this enlightening book, he shared something that indeed worked for him in his largest roles. He wrote that he employed *"an early morning meeting of my direct reports and principal aides that I called 'Morning Prayers'...just start the day together. It was a large meeting; as many as forty people attended. I had very strict rules:*

- *My morning meeting will never run longer than thirty minutes, usually less, so we can all get to work.*
- *This is the way we start the day as a team. I want you all to see me and check my morale and whether I seem okay. I*

> *want to look around the room at each of you and discern any subtle signals suggesting something I need to probe.*
> - *This is not a show-and-tell meeting. If you have nothing to say, don't speak.*
> - *No one gets reamed out here. We are sharing with each other, talking about the needs of the day and what we need to do, discussing how to fix problems. If anyone has really screwed up and needs counseling, we'll do it later, alone, in my office.*
> - *You will leave this meeting knowing what is on my mind, and therefore, had better be on your mind. I want each of you to meet with your staff to share with them what we have discussed. We need to connect from top to bottom.*
> - *And oh by the way, you can tell your spouse and relatives that you see the Secretary every day."*

I think this worked for Mr. Powell because of the discipline and consistency inherent in its structure, driven by a respect for its attendees. The meeting was held every day. It was never more than 30 minutes. It was never filled with "filler". It was authentic.

I also think it worked because of the transparency of its purpose. Mr. Powell understood the value in having his staff see him and for him to see them. He did not use the forum to address things best addressed elsewhere. There was value in letting people know how he was feeling, to get to know him and connect with him. It was organically part of his communication structure.

The key point is this: leadership is effective when your team feels connected to you and your organization's purpose. It is effective when the people on your team respect you and feel respected. It is effective when they know what's important to you and can clearly relay that to others.

To me, a relationship is most valuable when it is genuine. How much easier is it to pick up the phone and ask a favor from someone that you have a relationship with versus someone you do not? In the former, there's an inherent level of trust and you don't think twice about making or receiving that phone call; in the latter, the likelihood that those requests will be successful is lower, and are more apt to be treated as transactional and of lower priority.

Bill Hidell has been at various times in our relationship a colleague, a manager and a friend. Bill is one of the most naturally outgoing and sociable people I've ever known, quite gifted at carrying a conversation. While we haven't worked together in over fifteen years, I can count on him to regularly call me on the phone to check in and see how I'm doing. I imagine he does this regularly with a slew of folks in his network because that's how important connecting with others is to him.

As a manager, years ago, Bill saw me diligently working, and regularly implored me to step away from my desk and "go grab coffee" with people around the company to grow and develop my network. This did not come as naturally to me as it did Bill. Initially, I considered it a waste of time and a barrier to getting things done.

In fact, as he knew, it was a practical way to build and nurture relationships. How much easier is it to ask someone for help when you already have a connection with that person? Relationships drive results, and besides they make work more enjoyable.

I think deep down I knew that building a network was important, and I started to make the effort. It was tough at first because I was worried the networking would seem superficial, but it didn't need to be if I was authentic and curious. Making the effort paid off, and both my network and productivity got larger as a result.

Decades later, coffee (and intentional relationships) moved to the forefront again. Leading an organization of around 70 or so employees, I had to adjust how I interacted with the team. There were obviously a handful of folks that I needed to meet quite regularly with, even multiple times a day. It wasn't logistically possible, though, to give every employee the same treatment. Enter *Coffee with Paul,* a time that I set aside to bring small groups, maybe five-to-eight folks at a time, from my organization together to talk about anything the group was interested in. It could be personal or work-related, and the groups were free to ask me any question that was on their mind or share ideas they may have for improvement.

These *Coffees* provided a more conversational and less-intimidating environment than an all-hands meeting. Their informal and non-mandatory nature, and their regularity, allowed me to build trust and approachability, and I got to hear directly what was on the minds of those in my organization. I believe most of the participants felt like they were able to get to know me better, to connect with me, and learned that I genuinely cared about them and their feedback. I selfishly looked forward to these.

You can't spend equal time with everyone. It's not realistic. But the time you *do* spend with them must be the most important thing you're doing at that moment, without distractions. I strongly suggest putting your phone away, silencing email or messaging sounds, and be truly present with the person or people in front of you.

I've heard commentary in some spaces that being authentic doesn't work in interpersonal relationships. That clinging to your authentic self is unnecessarily rigid and could shut down the ability to connect with others. The arguments that landed, though, never seemed to be an indictment of *authenticity*, but rather extolled the virtues of relational flexibility and finding common ground, which to me have nothing to do with authenticity. Relating to others and adapting your interactions with them to make a connection is not being inauthentic. It's thoughtful relationship-building.

INTENTIONAL TONE-SETTING

David Kimm was a manager of mine for over a dozen years and a mentor for over twenty. His profoundly successful career has included C-level posts at multiple financial services institutions, and he is immensely respected in his field.

I am indebted to David for believing in me, for providing me with opportunities to grow and for giving me a years-long master class in tone setting. In meetings where he was not specifically designated as the primary speaker, David was frequently not the first person to speak. He was certainly never the loudest. Because he didn't interrupt others, he was seldom interrupted.

David often let the meeting come to him, and when he spoke, his tone, word choice and measured cadence of delivery made his opinion carry considerable weight. The pauses he took before leaning into a point he was about to make didn't feel performative, but thoughtful. It caused others to lean in in anticipation.

His ability in this area also tended to lower the temperature in the room. The way he did it was totally authentic to him, so it wasn't something I could emulate completely. I learned a lot by watching David in action, though. It was important for him in his role to keep an even keel, and though it probably came naturally to him, you could see how intentional he was and the impact it left.

Even long after we stopped working together, his example inspired me to continuously improve in this area. While I never approached David's excellence and made my share of missteps, my improved ability was noticed by others.

Cindy Willard is a risk professional I had the pleasure of working with at two companies over a half-dozen years.

In fact, it was Cindy who decided to reach out to me when I changed companies with an interest in joining me at my next stop. Cindy recently shared with me an experience from years ago that led to her decision:

During our time at a previous firm, we were in a particularly intense meeting…(where) emotions were high, and a few of us were deep in the heat of the moment, hashing out frustrations. You sat quietly for a while, just listening. At first, I wasn't sure why you hadn't jumped in.

When you finally spoke, you approached the conversation with a clear, emotion-free mindset. No blame. No defensiveness. You didn't escalate the tension—instead, you calmly brought us back to the core issue and re-centered the discussion around what needed to happen moving forward. It was a great example of what it means to lead with clarity and maturity, especially when things get uncomfortable. I wish I could remember what the issue even was, but because I can't, it also reminds me that what we think is a "big deal" often isn't. Here I am years later remembering your approach rather the actual "thing" itself.

What I appreciated most was how your approach left no room for personal attacks or finger-pointing. It shifted the tone of the room. People may have still been frustrated, but your ability to rise above the noise made it hard to argue with the logic of your points. That's real influence! … I filed it without ever forgetting it. It was that experience that compelled me to reach out to you when you left.

Jenn Byers is a professional with whom I worked over the last several years. A phenomenal person who is as talented as she is genuine, Jenn and I hit it off very early. I valued her from the minute we started working together. She recently validated my intentional efforts with an incredibly kind note:

> *You set the tone from the top. You were focused and hard-working, and you expected your teams to work hard. But you always cared about your people first – no matter how hard it got. We were people you valued to be a part of your team. You always asked how my day was, how my family was doing, how (her daughter's) volleyball tournaments were going – before we started discussing work. You even gave me recommendations for our family trip to the Outer Banks one year. Connecting with me as a person first motivated me even more to work harder for you as my leader.*

> *And you led with a powerful and collaborative approach that empowered your team. When we walked into a situation where there was acrimony amongst teams, I remember you saying 'we've got to change this culture.' You set the tone and it flowed through the entire project team, and we came out successful…because you led with a powerful and collaborative approach with an empowered team.*

Getting this type of reaction from others is tremendously gratifying. More importantly, it's validating to know that intentional effort in this area pays off. There's little chance that twenty-five-year-old me would have gotten this kind of feedback. I have the example set by other leaders to thank for that.

STANDING UP

Culture is protected when leaders take the heat, give air cover, and offer public support. These moments often mean more than any formal recognition because most people appreciate knowing their leaders have their back.

Amy Edmondson, in her terrific work *The Fearless Organization: Creating Psychological Safety in the Workplace for Learning, Innovation, and Growth*, wrote that psychological safety grows when people know their leader has their back. This means providing an environment where employees are comfortable speaking up without fear of negative consequences. Within the confines of the team, this fosters better idea sharing, innovation and learning. Outside of the team, it also means empowering your employees to challenge the status quo and publicly supporting and defending their words and actions.

When employees have come to me in recent years with a particularly thorny situation involving another leader, group or colleague, I often ask if they'd like me to go have the difficult conversation on their behalf. Because I have improved over the years at building an organization with the right people (more on that later), nine times out of ten, they decline the offer but move forward knowing that I have their back and will step in if necessary. In the rare instance where I'm taken up on the offer, we'll debrief afterward so he or she has the appropriate comfort level in the next difficult situation.

Lastly, standing up for your people includes actions when they're not in the room: advocating for them, praising their work…even shielding them from some of the noise and nonsense so they don't have to. I had an employee once write to me after I moved on from the group, "I now see…the amount of blocking and tackling you did for us. From the very bottom of my heart, THANK YOU! I have a whole new view and perspective on the number of things you did for us that we were not aware of; it has certainly not gone unnoticed!"

INTENTIONAL LEADERSHIP TAKES WORK

Being an intentional leader takes effort. It takes thoughtfulness, preparedness and a desire to do a little extra at times. It's not always easy, and it requires energy, presence, and repetition. Over time, it does become naturally and routinely part of who you are.

For instance, try to learn about what else is going on in people's lives and remember that they, in fact, have them. Ask leading questions and listen intently to what he or she has to say. Offer to be a mentor and put work into those relationships. Want a bonus idea? Put chocolate in a bowl on the desk in your office. People will be more inclined to come in, sit down and tell you what's on their mind if there's a fun reason to come in (hat tip: my mom).

Here's another example where I learned from a misstep. I had a particularly difficult relationship with an employee years ago that started poorly and never got better. The situation we were in was difficult, and neither of us made much of an effort to improve. One day, he came to my office, clearly disturbed. Among his list of grievances that day? "My birthday came and went and you never said a word." That one took me aback. I had no idea when his birthday was, or anyone else's. No one gave me a list of birthdays.

It also never occurred to me to ask for one...

The relationship in question here was not something that was going to be resolved by birthday wishes. I get that. Many people don't care about the day they were born after age 21. Upon reflection, however, I realized what's important is making a connection with the people around you and showing them you care about them. I had a golden opportunity to make someone feel good with a simple gesture that with preparation would require minimal effort. Since then, I have made sure to have an updated list of birthdays in my organization. I create a yearly calendar entry to remind me, and send a short, simple and personal message to them each year letting them know I'm thinking about them. Small gesture, but it feels good to do it.

People do notice this effort, as they would if you brought a homemade dessert to a potluck versus something in prepackaged plastic. Their effort tends to match yours in the long run.

Finally, it's a good idea to take the time to intentionally thank people for their impact and contributions to your success. Marv Adams was a top-flight executive who was my boss for a little over a year. Marv had succeeded at the highest level at multiple Fortune 500 stops, both inside and outside of financial services. He provided me with a different vantage point as an executive than I was accustomed to, and routinely got me out of my comfort zone. During our time together, we had really meaningful conversations about life, work and leadership. Though he led an organization enormous in size, when he spoke with me, he was thoughtful, he was direct and he listened.

Marv once told me how he had prepared for his first CIO role. He recalled reading everything he could get his hands on regarding how to succeed in that capacity, and being super-intentional about what he built and how he built it. While these were not foreign concepts to me at all, I hadn't employed them properly in my opportunity working for him. That was why he was sharing this with me.

Marv also gave me some very pointed and accurate feedback on areas where I could improve. My attempts at framing for him the difficulties of our situation very clearly came across as complaining, defeatist and pessimistic (I believe the actual comparison was Eeyore from Winnie the Pooh). He was right.

It's one thing to frame your situation as a method of articulating how you're going to solve for it. It's quite another to merely lament it, which is what it looked like I was doing. Nothing worthwhile in work or life is easy. I inherited an opportunity, not a problem. I was framing it as a problem. Even twenty years into my career, I wasn't expertly self-aware.

Objectively and in the moment, my time working for Marv would not be considered a success. That being said, I gathered so much experience from him and from that period of time. I was able to draw on those lessons in future roles when the compounding growth of my learning and experience began to show. Framed that way, it was one of the more important and necessary stops in my career, one that led to plenty of wins down the road.

Five years after speaking with him for the last time, I re-connected with Marv on LinkedIn for the sole purpose of thanking him. I told him that I had been reflecting on the opportunity I had to work with him, and that it was remarkable how much I gained from it professionally. I went on to tell him how much he helped me grow in my leadership journey, and that I'd seen the results of that growth in subsequent roles.

I really wanted him to understand how much of an impact he'd had on me. I had nothing to gain from reaching out to him. We had both moved on to different companies in different industries, and no longer traveled in the same circles. Marv quickly responded: "Paul, thanks for sharing that with me. That type of influence is what motivates me and keeps me going professionally. It sure isn't the politics and tactical operating pressures of executive roles that motivate me...I really appreciate you reaching out!" It felt as good for me to tell him what I told him as it probably did for him to hear it.

I became a better leader because of Marv, and the remainder of my career benefited from his presence. The main point here is to stress the importance of showing gratitude to those around you, that they know you care more about them as people than their title or job description.

As Maya Angelou famously said, *"People may forget what you said, but they'll never forget how you made them feel."*

Reflection Prompts

- When was the last time I made a first impression that truly reflected who I am as a leader?
- How well do the people on my team feel seen, heard, and supported by me?
- Am I spending my relational energy on the right people and moments, or just the loudest or most urgent?
- Where am I setting the tone unconsciously rather than intentionally?
- Who in my life or career deserves a message of thanks for their impact on me?

Intentional Actions

- Start a birthday or personal milestones list and send a short message each time. Set a recurring reminder.
- Schedule your own "Coffee With [You]" sessions. Start with a single small group and listen more than you talk.
- Send a note of gratitude to a former boss, mentor, or peer who shaped your leadership.
- Record and reflect on how you showed up in your last 3 meetings. Were you aligned with your intentions?

Closing Thoughts: Leading from the Inside Out

Amid the constant noise in our careers, we're often taught to lead by looking outward: at goals, performance metrics, budgets and organizational charts. Real leadership, the kind that endures and transforms, always begins inward.

The three chapters you've just read – on self-awareness, purpose, and intentional leadership – aren't theoretical. They're the foundation. They shape how we show up when things get hard, how we make decisions when no one's watching, and how we earn trust when trust matters most.

If you've been in leadership for any length of time, you know this: people don't just respond to what you say. They respond to what you value. And values aren't expressed through posters on a wall or one-off speeches—they show up in tone, timing, habits, and the behaviors you choose to reinforce. That's why this internal work matters so much.

Self-awareness helps us understand the ripple we leave behind in rooms we've exited. Purpose gives us the conviction to say yes to what aligns – and no to what doesn't. Intentionality helps us bring that conviction to life with empathy and consistency. Without those three, leadership becomes reactive, surface-level and performative.

With them? We become the kind of leader others trust enough to follow, not because we're perfect, but because we're present. Because we've done the work to know what we stand for, and we act like it.

Good leaders have credibility in their organization and with their peers. They build that credibility by choosing their words thoughtfully and purposefully. Good leaders are authentic, approachable and act with humility. They strive to be steady and consistent in their message and temperament. Good leaders are advocates for the people in their organization, while holding their teams and, more importantly, themselves accountable.

As you pause here before heading into the next section, I'd encourage you to take a breath. Revisit your notes or reflections. What has stuck with you? What made you nod in recognition, or squirm in discomfort?

Both are signs you're learning. And that's the whole point.

If you want to lead others well, you have to start by leading yourself well.

PART II: THE OUTER WORK

Building Aligned Culture and Strategy from the Start

Chapter 4:

Anatomy of a Successful Organization

I was well into my concurrent journeys of self-awareness and observing leadership traits in others when I started managing other people. It took some time to apply those learnings properly and intentionally align them with building culture. At first, I naively approached my responsibilities as transactional, viewing them solely through the lens of execution. I wasn't connecting my team's work with our purpose or direction because I hadn't created any purpose to connect it to.

Fortunately, I had leaders and mentors along the way that saw my potential and gave me opportunities to learn the right way. I know not everyone is so fortunate.

In time, I improved in self-awareness, personal purpose and intentionality – "The Inner Work" – that we covered in Part I of this book. These are foundational leadership capabilities that come from within.

From there, I needed to turn that foundation outward, develop a model that worked for me and refine it through experience. Part II of this book explores how great leaders shape culture, build strategy, and structure their teams to thrive - "The Outer Work." As you might guess, this happens intentionally, building on the skills and disciplines established through "The Inner Work."

It starts with understanding what makes a high-performing, successful organization in order to build and actively nurture each component in a thoughtful, purposeful way.

WHY GREAT TEAMS FEEL DIFFERENT

There is a certain *feeling* you get when you are part of a high-performing, successful organization. Maybe you can't put your finger on it, but you know. Conversely, there's a feeling when you're not. Does your team get things done or does it spin? Are barriers met with a problem-solving attitude or with hopelessness? Do other teams look to yours as the solution to their problems and want to know your perspectives? Or are you cordoned off and ignored? Do team members see problems as opportunities to solve them together or as groundwork for future blame?

I can go on. The point is that successful organizations don't just happen. The foundation is purposefully laid and carefully cultivated. Grasping this important truth was necessary for me. First, to learn how to start building it, then to articulate it in a way that was authentic to me and resonated with my leadership teams.

I consumed plenty of visuals and explanations of this concept over the years, tinkered with them and ultimately have used the following visual with my teams for the last decade-and-a-half:

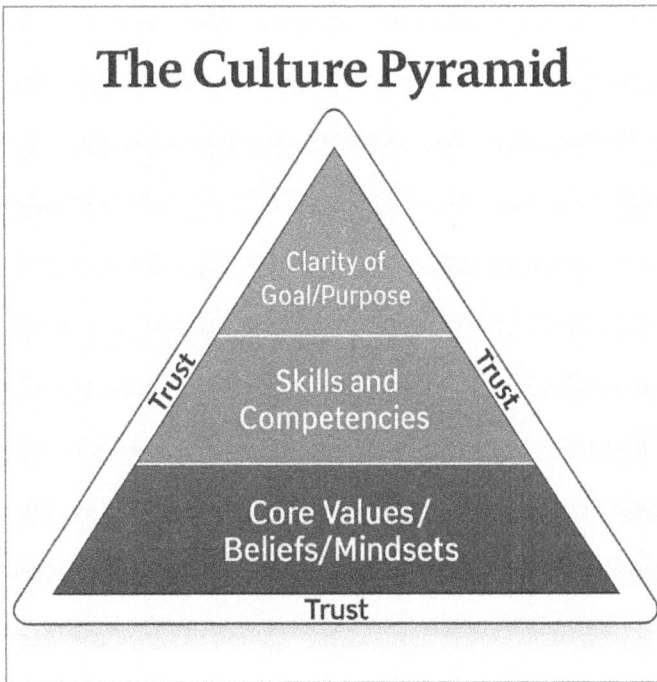

The Culture Pyramid

Clarity of Goal/Purpose

Skills and Competencies

Core Values/ Beliefs/Mindsets

Trust

Trust

Trust

Figure 4-1

This diagram shows the ingredients I believe to be crucial to a successful organization that has the right culture. It encompasses the characteristics its individual members bring to the team that are deeply ingrained in who they are as people, as well as those they're still building upon. It also includes how clear the purpose and goals of the organization are to all of its members, and the trust that permeates from ideas to action.

CORE VALUES, BELIEFS AND MINDSETS

The most basic and foundational components of an excellent team are the core values, beliefs and mindsets each member brings with them. These were formed in each person long before he or she set foot on the team. They are the unseen drivers of what each person is all about, their character.

At this level of the pyramid, a leader has very little impact on these traits; they are core to each person, but they do need to align with the true north of the team and its leader in order for the team to be successful. Especially since each member's behaviors are primarily driven by these core inherent qualities.

As a result, hiring and retaining the right people is of utmost importance. In corporate America, the cost of a poor hire is staggering. From a direct cost perspective, there's the cost of recruiting and onboarding them, the cost of paying them during their tenure and the cost of letting them go. The indirect costs are potentially more harmful. The management time of more active supervision and of "managing them out" is taxing. The hit to your team's reputation can be potentially severe, and the opportunity cost of not being able to use those resources elsewhere can be quite regrettable. Worst of all, the hit to your team's morale and sustainable productivity can severely diminish its success and you could lose core talent.

That's why the recruitment and interview processes are so important. This is the time when you must discern whether a potential hire, at their core, is aligned with your organization's core values.

Face-to-face interviews, if at all possible, have to be part of the process. Ask values-based questions, such as:

> *"Tell me about a situation when you faced a moral dilemma at work, and how you handled it?"*

> *"What motivates you at work? Give me an example when your motivation helped you succeed in a challenging situation."*

> *"Describe a time when you disagreed with a colleague or manager. How did you handle the situation?"*

I'd like to say that simply asking these questions, and digesting the responses to them, is the ticket to a 100 percent hiring success rate. It's not. There is a certain feel that comes with experience that will also aid you. To minimize bias and sample size issues, you should certainly employ multiple interviewers. Make sure to give each interviewer something specific to look for, and compare notes after.

Referrals from people you trust, and who themselves align with your core values, can also be helpful. Once you have surrounded yourself with aligned leaders who have proven to have good eyes for fit, you may feel comfortable stepping back from interviews for certain roles further down into your organization. Until you have the utmost comfort here, it's best to stay involved. Again, the cost of getting it wrong is high.

SKILLS AND COMPETENCIES

Moving to the middle tier of the pyramid, we come to the skills and competencies of each member and in aggregate. This is far less static than core values. Each person brings a set of skills and competencies to the team and their role, and they are always growing and evolving as they learn lessons and gain proficiency.

There is certainly a requisite set of skills and/or competencies that are must haves in order to fill most roles. The dynamic nature of a skill set makes this area less of an exact science at the individual level. Understanding where individual growth opportunities exist and are worth investing in is crucial, a topic we'll cover in a bit more detail later in this chapter.

When hiring or building teams, it's best not to only look for talent in isolation (though there may be times when a specific skill is necessary). Instead, consider how one person's strengths may amplify others. You're not just filling a seat, but shaping a puzzle.

Competency stacking is the idea that a team's performance is elevated by how talents interact and complement each other, not just individual talents in a vacuum.

Instead of hiring someone purely because he or she checks a specific box (e.g., "we need someone who knows SQL"), you hire based on how the skill set fills *a capability gap*, supports *team cohesion*, or multiplies *others' effectiveness*. A stacked team avoids skill silos and allows for increased coverage, more collaboration and less key-person risk.

In aggregate, the team's skills and competencies carry a lot of importance of course. Fitting all of these together as pieces in a puzzle is a fun challenge for any leader, because the skills possessed and needed are constantly changing.

While we're on this topic, I should note that thriving organizations aren't built solely by adding new skill sets. Certain situations call for it, but it can be stifling to growth and costly over time. Instead, they're often built by wisely combining acquired talent with intentional organic growth. Before hiring, ask: Do we need to hire this capability *from outside*, or do we already have the seed of capability here with someone who just needs the right opportunity to grow?"

In her book *Multipliers*, Liz Wiseman explains the virtue of leaders who optimize talent by creating growth opportunities, empowering their members to be accountable, while encouraging risk taking. These leaders are more apt to create high-performing teams, teams marked by a penchant for attracting and retaining above-average talent.

Rather than always filling capability gaps by hiring externally, emphasize growing skills within your existing team. Doing so can increase engagement and loyalty because the staff sees you're investing in them. The likely result of lower attrition means you'll preserve institutional knowledge, which is deployed faster and cheaper than onboarding a new hire. It also creates more agility on your team, meaning you can pivot more easily when the situation calls for it.

How might you do this in practice?

Stretch assignments, which are projects or tasks beyond someone's responsibility and slightly beyond their current skills, are one way. Let a mid-level analyst lead a cross-functional project, and pair them with someone to coach them through it. Shadowing is another. For example, pair a risk professional with an operations or sales lead for a quarter to allow both sides to get a better understanding of how their respective priorities and processes intersect, complement and conflict with one another. This "walk in their shoes" action is also a great way to get cross-organizational teams to become closer.

Lastly, because not all advancement is vertical and linear, you can create informal pathways or alternative development lanes for your team members. This allows them to grow laterally by gaining supplemental knowledge or adding complementary skills or competencies that prepare them for their next upward career step. A former executive colleague of mine used to say of career advancement that thinking of it as a *ladder* is not always optimal. Sometimes approaching it as *lattice* is the best path to growth."

CLARITY OF GOAL AND PURPOSE

Atop the pyramid is an environment where everyone on the team, as well as those adjacent to or depending on it, has clarity of the team's goals (both philosophical and business-centric) and its purpose. While everyone plays a role in this clarity, responsibility for this lies squarely with its leader.

As we mentioned in Chapter 2, understanding goal and purpose gives everyone something to connect to. It enables the team to move confidently, knowing why they're here and how the work they're doing is connected to the big picture. It also helps team members prioritize work, and sometimes decline work, that doesn't align with the organization's goals and purpose.

When a team's goals and purpose are measured, socialized and known outside of the team, it offers an opportunity for a transparent, "no surprises" engagement model that demystifies what is "in bounds" and "out of bounds," or at least gives sound reasoning behind a team's activities and prioritization.

Over the last decade-plus, I have had a number of opportunities to bring this to life and it starts with laying some groundwork. I frequently refer to Michael Watkins' *The First 90 Days* for guidance. As part of my onboarding, I embark on an extensive listening tour to gain a deeper understanding of where the organization stands and where it needs to go. I then validate that understanding using Watkins' STaRS model: Start-up, Turnaround, Realignment, Sustaining Success.

I perform a SWOT Analysis, which helps inform the beginning of the organizational strategy by calling out strengths, weaknesses, opportunities and threats. I map out how things currently get done, both internally and externally. I also document organizational pathways – such as who holds formal and informal power, who defers to whom, where bottlenecks exist, and where strategic alignment or trust issues appear. I will update these, over time, as necessary. Then, following Watkins' lead, I confirm the following with my boss through intentional dialogue:

- Agreement on my assessment of the situation
- Agreement on expectations and success measures
- Optimal interaction model with one another and understanding style differences
- Resources necessary for success
- How we can use this role to aid in my personal development in a way that helps the organization

With all of that relatively concrete, I write down the organization's mission and vision from my perspective. I share this with my leadership team with context, get their feedback and edit or augment the mission and vision where warranted.

I then take five strategic cultural themes that I've consistently carried with me for a long time, adjust them to properly align to the current situation and company verbiage, and extensively discuss these with my leadership team and ultimately the organization as a whole. We'll cover these themes in the next two chapters.

All of these documents serve as a skeletal structure to how I'll communicate our purpose, our "true north," repeatedly and in an accessible way for the remainder of my tenure. I'll do so in structured and unstructured ways.

In a more structured way, my messages regarding our purpose and goals weave through these documents as part of my kickoff speeches, all-hands meetings and strategic leadership workshops. The consistency from quarter-to-quarter and year-to-year is a helpful and consistent anchor for the team.

Perhaps more important are the unstructured or organic ways of intentional connections. These can be through situational decision-making, conflict-settling, recognition and discipline. For instance, intentionally saying, "Our primary purpose is to help this organization become better at managing its risk. Adding this proposed step in our process to satisfy someone else's priorities doesn't help us do that, so we're not going to" anchors my actions to our purpose. That clarity makes these moments more meaningful, tethered to a shared purpose rather than my personal preference. And even if the other parties disagree or would have done it differently, they could at least respect my decision or perspective because it was grounded in our shared understanding of what was important.

Patrick Lencioni's impactful book *The Advantage* is quite relevant here. In that work, Lencioni says that organizational health is required for success. Of his Four Disciplines of Organizational Health, three of the four have to do with clarity: creating it, overcommunicating it and reinforcing it.

It's when your team has this clarity - combined with the requisite core beliefs, values, skills and competencies - that you can become more coach than problem-solver, that you can empower others to think and act on their own, that you can focus on lowering barriers, removing bottlenecks and building better systems.

TRUST AS THE INTEGRATOR

The magic ingredient that is like motor oil to an engine is trust. While it is certainly earned over time, it can be accelerated by having a team containing all of the other elements of the pyramid. It's perhaps best represented as four facets of organizational trust, where each person in that organization could answer affirmatively about someone else, and vice-versa:

1. **Competency Trust**: I trust you will do your job, and that you have the appropriate skills and competencies.
2. **Reliability Trust**: I trust you'll do what you say, that you will hold up your end of the bargain, and that if you don't, you'll own it and improve.

3. **Character Trust**: I trust your motives and ethics are true and aligned with our core values, beliefs and mindsets.
4. **Psychological Trust**: I trust this is a safe space for honesty, mistakes, and ideas, based on positive intent. I trust that if something impedes my progress that I will get leadership and/or colleague support to get back on track.

In *The Fearless Organization* Amy Edmondson argues that psychological safety, created through trust, is crucial for teams and companies to thrive. It's not that it creates a more enjoyable environment to work in, though it does. The bigger point for organizational success is that trust leads to speed – in learning, decision-making, problem-solving, innovation, agility and resilience.

When all of this is in place, it becomes easier to empower your employees, and easier for them to feel empowered. It's also easier for them to start each week saying, "I *get* to do this with my team.". For your employees, there are few more comforting feelings than knowing they're in this together; few worse or lonelier than feeling like it's them against the world. That's why trust is so important.

We discussed "misalignment" in Chapter 2 and "standing up" for your team in Chapter 3. I want to emphasize in this section on "trust" how important these concepts are to your team's success and its culture. Consistency and transparency regarding alignment with core beliefs is vital, and that includes how dedicated you and the team are at correcting when necessary.

As a leader, what you tolerate will build or erode trust on your team. When they see that you won't tolerate a lack of core beliefs or poor performance, and you actively rectify it, trust goes up. When you let it slide, so does their trust. Have you ever been on a team with a bad actor whose behavior drags the team down? It's aggravating. When that behavior isn't addressed, aggravating turns to infuriating, which turns to disengagement.

Same goes for poor planning, decisions or execution, yours included. While mistakes are inevitable, how you show up when they occur will impact team culture and morale. Acknowledging the error, committing to resolving it and following through will build trust and strengthen alignment. So will expecting the same from your team.

BUILD AROUND THE BEST

Every team contains multiple people, ideally structured with complementary skills and competencies to achieve the team's goals that ideally become greater than the sum of its parts. The larger the team, the bigger the puzzle; still, the concept is a rather simple and consistent one.

When it comes to being a high-performing team rooted in the right culture, how you build the team requires extra intentionality and care, because a strong culture is one that grows organically.

I've come to look for five traits in the individuals on any team I lead:

1. Do they understand our organization's systems and processes, culture and values?
2. Is their outlook generally optimistic and do they motivate others driven by that optimism?
3. Are they excellent communicators (verbal and written)?
4. Do they have a track record of accountability?
5. Are they naturally curious with a bias for action?

It's not realistic to expect everyone in your organization to possess all five of these traits. There will certainly be people that are solid contributors while having fewer than five.

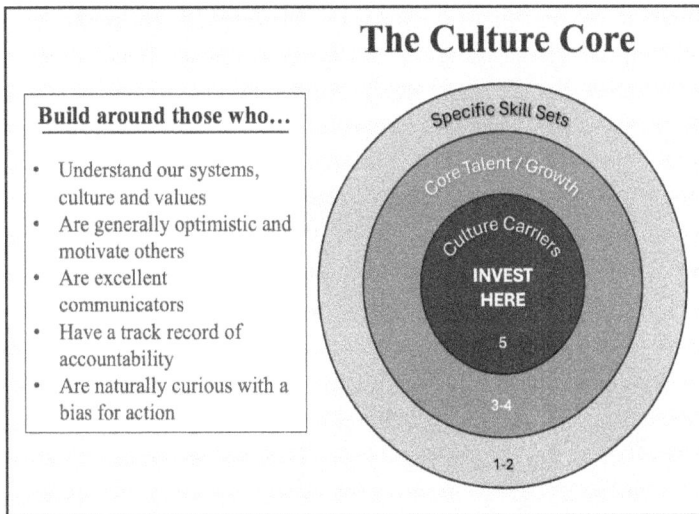

The Culture Core

Build around those who...

- Understand our systems, culture and values
- Are generally optimistic and motivate others
- Are excellent communicators
- Have a track record of accountability
- Are naturally curious with a bias for action

Specific Skill Sets

Core Talent / Growth

Culture Carriers

INVEST HERE

5

3-4

1-2

Figure 4-2

For instance, you may need a specific skill set on your team. It's quite possible that, given the right set of responsibilities, a person with a track record of accountability and an understanding of your organization's systems, culture and values can be successful in helping your team meet its goal and purpose. He or she may fill an important niche and be in a role that they're happy in, with no desire to advance. There will be circumstances where that's perfectly fine.

I do believe, however, that your organization's sustainable success is positively correlated with the percentage of folks that possess at least four.

And those that have all five?

Invest in these employees' careers and their growth. Challenge them. Support them. Pay them. Ideally, they will appear throughout your organization at all levels, not just among your direct reports. These people are your leadership pipeline.

They are also your **Culture Carriers**. Not only will they be your highest performers, they will have an infectious impact on those around them. Those in the concentric circles as shown above that are drawn to leadership qualities will naturally be influenced by the traits of those that carry them. As you understand their areas of interaction and influence, they can be a spokesperson for you, as appropriate, when you're not in the room. Because of the multiplying value they can provide, you want to position these Culture Carriers throughout your organization so they can influence outward.

Reflection Prompts

- How clearly can each member of my team articulate the organization's purpose and goals?
- When was the last time I assessed whether my team's structure aligns with its mission?
- Am I intentionally investing in existing team members' development or defaulting to hiring externally?
- How am I currently identifying and empowering Culture Carriers in my organization?
- Where might trust be breaking down across my team, and why?

Intentional Actions

- Ask each person on your team to describe your mission, vision, and top priorities.
- Create a visual map of your team's current skills and competencies, and identify gaps or overlaps.
- Pilot a stretch assignment program—identify 1–2 individuals who could up-skill with a new challenge.
- Hold a Culture Carrier roundtable to hear from those who exemplify your core values and mindset.
- Use the four facets of trust (competency, reliability, character, psychological) to evaluate team dynamics.

Chapter 5:

Design For Purposeful Alignment

As I mentioned earlier, I didn't approach my early managerial responsibilities as much more than transactional. As my responsibilities grew, I brought others in to help. But at the time, I mistakenly saw them as task-driven extensions of myself. "Me"-centric instead of "We"-centric. Wrong way to approach it, I know, but eventually I learned the power of collectively pursuing a common purpose. I also learned that the long-term momentum that comes from having your team buy into that common purpose dwarfs that which comes from a collection of transactional task masters.

I started to form themes in my head that meant the most to me and gradually brought them to life. For quite some time now, I have grounded myself in five strategic cultural themes, which remain the same and are adjusted slightly to align to each situation and organization that I've led. These form the basis for instilling the appropriate culture and performance expectations; first with my leadership team, and ultimately the organization as a whole. They are my anchors, reference points and sanity checks, all in one.

Each theme guides the team in the direction I want to take it, and is open-ended enough for us to collectively solidify what it means to make that theme stick. From there, we have an easier path to set meaningful and measurable performance goals that align with our direction.

Grounding my teams in these themes, to me, is more impactful than mission or vision statements alone. Those statements are important, and there is value in their pithiness. For me, these themes lead to action in a more meaningful way.

A representative slide for each theme is included in the following pages. Each slide begins with my personal assertions about that theme, includes a quote that serves as a guidepost and ends with a series of reflection questions.

These are the five themes that work for me – a financial services risk management executive. While I believe much of what drives me here transcends financial services or risk management, you may find that your five are slightly different, or the way you bring them to life is different. If so, that's terrific! What's important is that you have something authentic to you that works. Hopefully this gets the juices flowing.

ESTABLISHING CULTURE WITH THE TEAM

Now that we've defined the foundational elements of a healthy culture, the next step is to architect it and help everyone row in the same direction. The goal is to have an aligned group that operates in an efficient, well-managed way.

Where else to start, but by clearly defining the organization's north star? Teams that operate with one can focus on the right problems and opportunities more easily. And there's a certain magic of seeing people at every level of the organization state with pride how their job specifically aligns with an organizational goal. By overtly stating who it is that we want to be, it'll be easier to establish expectations, set priorities and fill the team with the right people.

Our Culture

We provide expertise, and prioritize action and common sense. We help our business partners understand "why" and make risk management as easy as possible.	
Guidepost	*"When you're surrounded by people who share a passionate commitment around a common purpose, anything is possible."* -Howard Shultz, Executive Chairman, Starbucks
Reflection Questions	• Is our team empowered and enabled, with clarity of goal & purpose? • Do we have inherent trust, and where do we need to build it? • Are we always striving to be better? • How adept is the team at adapting to change? Leading change? • Do we have a positive team mindset modeling the right behavior? • What do we hope to be? How is that different than what we are now? • Are we consistently reinforcing and offering guidance on our purpose – internally AND externally?

Figure 5-1

This foundation is the beginning of the culture we intend to grow and nurture. Of the five themes, the underpinnings of **"Our Culture"** are more of an organic extension of the concepts in Chapter 4, which is by design, and allows for a natural transition from what we believe to be important to how we aim to grow our organizational culture intentionally.

I believe that risk management as a discipline is not particularly complicated. After building risk programs and integrating them into business operations and systems for decades, however, I have observed the following phenomenon: it's the companies and people that tend to make it complicated. This is probably also true in other disciplines.

Since risk management is not a revenue producer, it's imperative that it's managed as efficiently as possible. I'm very passionate about meeting business leaders where they are, speaking in their terms and approaching risk-related manners as practically as possible. When it's done well, risk management happens naturally in the course of running your business. When it's not, it can be as costly as it is ineffective.

Because of this passion, I want to instill a certain culture in any organization I'm fortunate to lead. In this instance, I want us to help organizations be successful by allowing them to easily integrate risk into their day-to-day, make better decisions and be well-managed. When they're successful, we're successful. To do that, we'll bring expertise and a consultation mindset, prioritize action over talk, common sense over nonsense and we'll demystify risk and make it easier to do in a way that leads to efficient and effective programs. This is my starting point.

The **"Our Culture"** Reflection Questions in Figure 5-1 are also starting points for our own reflection and to prompt conversation and action-taking for the leadership team as a whole. Depending on where the organization is on our maturity continuum, these can be start-from-scratch aspirational questions or they can be checkpoints of progress.

For example, if this is a new build of a team, then we already know the answer to most of the Reflection Questions, and the answer is either "no" or "not yet". If we haven't shared our purpose and our goals, then they obviously won't have that clarity.

Still, these questions lead us to articulate our purpose to business partners, other leaders and potential new hires. Over time, we might use a question like, "How adept is the team at adapting to or leading change?" in benchmarking or performance management at the individual and team level.

Lastly, it's important to note that part of building a culture is setting expectations and managing them consistently. I want professionals on my team that are good at what they do, are easy to do business with, that are accountable and follow through on what they say. I won't tolerate unprofessional behavior, or excuses.

CAPABILITIES WITH CONTEXT

Sitting squarely in the middle of the Culture Pyramid in Chapter 4 are "Skills and Competencies". This Strategic Cultural Theme, **"Our Capabilities"**, incorporates that important concept and takes it a step further. It's not simply whether the individuals on the team and the team as a whole have the necessary skills and competencies, though that's certainly a big part of it. On top of that is whether the team is *capable* of achieving our objectives in the manner that aligns with our culture. That distinction can take several forms.

Our Capabilities

Our entire team must be capable of operationalizing our purpose, and we must maximize our skills and competencies in a well-managed way.	
Guidepost	*"No horse gets anywhere until he is harnessed. No stream or gas drives anything until it's confined. No Niagara is ever turned into light and power until it is tunneled. No life ever grows great until it is focused, dedicated, disciplined."* -Harry Emerson Fosdick, Pastor/Writer
Reflection Questions	• Can everyone on our team articulate "why"? • Are our colleagues capable of making decisions? • Data, analytics and reporting is no longer the future of risk management. It is the now. How can we improve here? • Are we hiring and developing fungible skills and capabilities and following through on use of that fungibility?

Figure 5-2

Again, the reflection questions help us define where to apply intentional focus to ensure we are as well-managed an organization as possible. Using my recent organizations – in financial services risk management – as the continuing example, our focus was in four areas.

First, as we articulated in **"Our Culture"**, we need our business partners to understand the "why" behind our mission and the "why" of risk management. In order to do that, though, our own team needs to know "why" and also be capable of articulating it. That may be easier at the higher levels of the organization, and more questionable as we move through all levels of the team.

This is, of course, important if you want your team to successfully interact with and influence others. There's a bigger, longer-lasting reason. In Simon Sinek's *Start with Why* he discusses his "Golden Circle" concept. He says that everyone can tell you what they do, some can tell you how they do it, but far fewer know why (aside from profit, which is an outcome, not a purpose). Sinek says people don't buy what you do, they buy why you do it. In his example, he's speaking of customers. It also applies to your organization.

Going back to last section, I stated that our goal is to help organizations be successful by allowing them to easily integrate risk into their day-to-day, make better decisions and be well-managed. When they're successful, we're successful. To do that, we'll bring expertise and a consultation mindset, prioritize action over talk, common sense over nonsense and we'll demystify risk and make it easier to do in a way that leads to efficient and effective programs. The purpose is visible.

We can't start with "we'll document and report on operational losses in a timely manner" because that's a "what". Instead, we can say that we help businesses easily integrate risk into their day-to-day, make better decisions and be well-managed ("why"), that operational losses help us learn where processes or controls need improvement ("how") and that documenting operational losses in a timely manner ("what") gives us the ability to learn and improve.

For the analyst doing the work, it's much more gratifying to say "I help my business make better risk decisions" than "I document operational losses." As a leader, it's important to make your purpose visible, articulate meaning, and connect initiatives, projects and daily work to strategic goals and purpose.

It's also important to repeat core tenets and tie them to matters at hand, being intentional in telling folks the "why" behind strategy and purpose, and the "why" behind your decision-making. Share as appropriate, of course, but the desired outcome is (on the positive) people will respect your willingness to share the why even if they may not agree with you, and (on the negative) you reduce the risk of people assuming why you're doing something, which often leads to cultural and performance drags on the team.

Second, if we've empowered and enabled our team members (and again building on **"Our Culture"**) to make decisions, they must be capable of actually doing so. We have to know that individual employees have the skill to make informed decisions, and address any shortcomings here. We're also asking if all of our leaders have built decision-making authority and clarity into their own operating models and behaviors. If our message from the top is that employees are empowered to make decisions, then their direct managers inconsistently apply that message in practice, it can negatively impact a team's production and culture. As Liz Wiseman said in *Multipliers*, "The best leaders are genius makers. They bring out the intelligence in everyone." If we've stocked our team with good, smart people, we want to take advantage of that, right?

Where the first two reflection questions overlap and intertwine with **"Our Culture"**, the third does so with **"Find a Better Way"**, which we'll dig into in the next chapter. Data, analytics and reporting, including robotics and AI, when used responsibly, can give managers the information they need to manage risk much more quickly and efficiently. It allows us to make the easy things easy, and devote more of our human capital to more advanced concepts or difficult decisions.

Finally, every team needs the right skills and competencies, including developing some measure of fungible skills across the team. This reflection question is aimed at developing a conscious approach to doing that, and then actually using that fungibility. Other questions to ask? Are we resorting primarily to hiring externally over a prolonged period? Do we fail to define internal career paths, do we have a blind spot regarding our talent that leads us to assume external is the way to go? Are we actively creating stretch assignments? These could all be red flags and opportunities to course correct.

DESIGNING THE OPTIMAL STRUCTURE

Well-run organizations are those that have the right people in the right roles doing the right work. Every well-run organization also has an optimal organizational structure. And every organization has optimal systems to share information and leverage skills. When done right all of these are in alignment.

I've led many organizations where we structured, or re-structured, based on the needs we had at the time, and at some point, those needs changed. In one situation, I led a group of risk professionals that interfaced with over a dozen large organizations across the company. Initially, I needed to create the right culture, mindset and operating systems so I hired and organized my team to solve for those priorities. After some time passed, and we had solved for or at least stabilized those priorities, we could focus on subject matter expertise gaps, fungible skills and bench.

The optimal structure is not a one-time design project. It's a living organism. When leaders treat structure as fixed, they risk stifling the very agility they hope to enable.

But the reason it's so important to regularly revisit **"Our Structure"** is that every one of these things as well as our environment and expectations, are constantly changing and evolving. When structure evolves, it also reshapes how we deploy and develop talent.

Our Structure

	Optimal structures are rooted in a common understanding of an organization's goals and purpose, and align with the right skills and processes.	
Guidepost	*"An aligned organization gets things done faster, with less effort, and with better results, and is more agile and responsive to changing business conditions."* *-Torben Rick, Business Improvement Executive/Writer*	
Reflection Questions	• What is the optimal structure that aligns staff with our goal and purpose? • Do we have the right mix of core competencies, specific skills and culture carriers? Are they aligned structurally to maximize team effectiveness? • Where are we falling short and need help? • What is our assessment of bench strength? • Is our communication strategy (internally and externally) fit for purpose?	

Figure 5-3

An org structure that was optimal two years ago may no longer be optimal today. That could be because the organization is capable of running leaner than two years ago due to improved systems. Maybe the organization failed to fully integrate a new product or process and the organizational model needs to be revisited. Or perhaps you're not fully leveraging complementary skill sets.

Remember the five traits to build around from last chapter: an understanding of our organization's systems and processes, culture and values; an optimistic and motivating personality, excellent communicator, a track record of accountability, naturally curious with a bias for action?

This is the time when we ask ourselves who on the team has all five traits – the Culture Carriers – and how can we best build around them. The answers are always changing.

Same goes with bench strength and attrition. There are certain roles on the team where the incumbent may need 18 months in seat to be proficient, and others that may only need 4-6 months. Managers need a firm grasp on all aspects of their bench and pipeline in order to maximize preparedness.

Lastly, there's the structure of your team's communications. This includes internal communications with your team, external communications with partner organizations and outward-facing communication external to your company. Each mode has different goals, and different optimal ways to achieve them.

But if you consistently set aside time to intentionally plan for communicating, you can integrate it into your systems and processes in a way that is natural, organized and effective. This applies everywhere, regardless of the other party to your communication.

Refer to the top of Figure 5-3: "Optimal structures are rooted in a common understanding of an organization's goals and purpose…" Think about times when things broke down – between you and your team, between you and your peers, or between your team and other teams. Was everyone involved armed with that common understanding? With your "why"? This is where being intentional really comes in handy. You can't assume because you told them once, that they instinctively remember. This is especially true with teams, where members change and don't always commit your goals and purpose to memory.

There are also formal and informal pathways to consider. Both are important and both work together dynamically.

Formal communication pathways are your established, official channels for communication. We use these to ensure there is clear, structured and consistent information flow. This is the "official stuff," established for posterity and to create transparency and accountability. Think staff meetings, policy communications, reports, intranet sites and feedback loops (vertical) as well as multi-team collaboration communications or project steering committees (horizontal). All of these are needed because of the structure, documentation and consistency they provide.

Careful planning and execution can make formal pathways work. There is considerably more structure here, and though it requires work, that work is a little more predictable. We've had some version of one-on-one meetings, leadership staff meetings, leadership strategy meetings, All-Hands meetings and Coffee with Paul (see Chapter 3) in addition to horizontal formal pathways.

Each internal communication needs to have a commonly understood specific purpose, with specific expectations, and they need to fit together in a complementary way. Again, we're never in a static environment. Not every aspect of our formal structure, content or delivery that works today will work next year, so we regularly revisit all of it.

Of course, we're all human beings, so we have to recognize the power of informal communication pathways. These are also a vital part of organizational culture, which can be a good or bad thing. This is the "unofficial stuff," the organic and unofficial communication that happens through impromptu dialogue in the moments between the formal communication pathways – an instant message, a quick conversation after a meeting or in the break room, or even a chat at happy hour. When employees bond and collaborate with others, it can be a powerful thing.

As a leader, and just one person, you can't possibly structure an inherently unstructured environment. You certainly can't be in all places to ensure consistency in message or a common understanding of goal and purpose. This is where the Culture Carriers can be super helpful.

You want as many people as possible to embody the culture you hope to build/maintain. Your Culture Carriers can be a proxy for you when you're not in the room, influencing those around them in an informal way that may resonate with those in their circles more effectively than even you could. Take care of these folks; they are the future.

Reflection Prompts

- How clearly can every member of my team explain our team's purpose, priorities, and role relative to the larger organization?
- What behaviors do we reward, and are they aligned with the culture we say we want?
- Where are we currently over- or under-indexed in terms of skills and capabilities?
- How often do we re-evaluate our structure?
- Are we optimally leveraging our culture carriers?

Intentional Actions

- Draft or revisit your version of "**Our Culture,**" "**Our Capabilities,**" and "**Our Structure.**" Share them with your team and workshop them together.
- Identify three high-potential team members and design a development or stretch opportunity that aligns with their goals and your organization's needs.
- Create a feedback channel to regularly gather team input on capability gaps or hidden blockers.
- Observe team communication flows for a month, formal and informal, and determine if they reinforce or undermine your intended culture.

Chapter 6:

Slow the Game Down

When we look at organizations, we often think of them instinctively as "well-managed" or "not well-managed". While we might less often discern why, the signs are clearly there. There was a time in my career where an organization I led had a working relationship with an organization in another part of the company. Our programs and operations were impacted by theirs, and our processes were designed as a result of their policies. The other organization always seemed to be scrambling and responding to the latest fire drill. Like any organization that is intertwined with another in a value stream, their fires became our fires all too frequently. "Sorry for the quick turnaround..." was a common intro to the latest emergency.

There was more. The organization at all levels seemed to prioritize talking at the expense of thinking or doing, and focused on "Monday Morning Quarterbacking" the past rather than designing and executing what could be. They didn't ask many questions or build relationships. Though they had templatized success criteria, they couldn't explain them, let alone defend them. Mostly, the game always seemed to be going just a bit too fast for them.

You've no doubt seen at least some of these characteristics throughout your career. Why are teams like this so commonplace? Sure, their processes or systems could be sub-optimal. Maybe the talent level isn't where it needs to be. But it can't be just process and talent. Perhaps those are symptoms rather than the cause. And I'm sure you've seen an organization that wasn't well-managed which prompted a change to be made at the top of the organization. Sometimes the organization turned around; sometimes it didn't. Why is that? Now we're getting closer to the real issue.

The final two of my five cultural themes step firmly into executing our purpose. Before we get to those, I'd like to share some important facets of what I like to call "slowing the game down."

Few concepts translate from sports to business as clearly as slowing the game down. In either arena, it is an outcome that happens when we employ "The Four P's."

PREPARATION

Derek Jeter once summarized it perfectly: "It slows down when you're prepared. It speeds up when you're unprepared." The best hitters in baseball typically spend more time studying, watching video and learning pitcher tendencies.

There's even an entire industry devoted to neuro-cognitive training for athletes to accelerate decision making by speeding up the processing of what the eyes see to how the brain acts – in effect, slowing the game down.

In business, preparation is beyond crucial in so many ways.

When Marv Adams was not-so-subtly telling me all that he did to understand what makes a successful CIO, he was impressing upon me the importance of preparation in being successful in a new job.

> ### *Preparation:*
> *Doing the work before the work so you can act and lead with mindfulness and clarity instead of scrambling and reacting.*

Making informed decisions is a key to all disciplines in business, so it's astounding how unprepared I've seen people in decision-making roles or committees with decision-making responsibilities. On the flip side, I've seen quintessential preparation first-hand.

Sue O'Donnell is one of the best leaders I had the opportunity to work with in my career. In her role as an operations executive leading an organization of over 1,200 people, Sue perfectly embodied a "no surprises" mentality, and I certainly appreciated her common-sense approach to problem-solving. She was a good person who attracted good people to work with her.

95

Also, she was always prepared.

Sue came to every important discussion or meeting armed with the information she needed to move to successful outcomes. She did that by thoughtfully calling on people close to that topic in advance to get context and hear their perspective. Plus, she read everything in sight. It didn't matter if committee materials were 600 pages in length, she read every page and was prepared to challenge when necessary. More than a few times, she successfully helped her company steer toward the right decision because she had the courage to speak up when others wouldn't.

That courage came from being prepared. Because she had studied an issue from all sides, gotten the perspective of smart people around her and done her homework, Sue was armed with knowledge that let her speak with authority and build guiding coalitions to the best course of action.

In a world where strategic risk can take down a company, leaders like Sue encapsulate all the good that comes from preparation.

PRIORITIZATION

I credit the period of my life where I passionately pursued distance running with helping me in other areas of my life, particularly my career. Over the course of about a dozen years, I was fortunate to run nine marathons (including three Boston Marathons), a 50-kilometer trail race, and countless 5K, 10K and half-marathon races along the way. I wanted to be a healthy role model for my young daughter and I was certainly interested in the physical benefits I got from running.

More importantly, perhaps the most enlightening part of that journey was how the goal-setting and discipline that it required easily translated into my work life. A natural part of that discipline was prioritization. If I wanted to run 60 miles per week without sacrificing family and career, I needed to do it at 5am or earlier. If I wanted to have successful long runs, track workouts or tempo runs at 5am, I needed to go to bed early, eat a proper diet and avoid alcohol. My day-to-day life needed discipline-driven prioritization. I intentionally opted for those things over others because they were aligned with my goals. They became habits.

Prioritization:
Purposefully focusing and spending your time on what matters most, so your energy goes to your reason for being instead of noise.

Sure enough, goal-setting, discipline and prioritization became more natural at work. I'm convinced that the connection here was not coincidental.

I mentioned Greg McKeon's book *Essentialism: The Disciplined Pursuit of Less* in Chapter 2 when discussing boundaries as a gift for your team. To be an essentialist is to recognize just how much in our world and work life is noise. Unimportant. Inconsequential. Ultimately, it means intentionally setting criteria for what is and isn't worth our time. I can't tell you how many times I've sat in a large meeting and ruminated on how much that meeting was costing the firm.

Prioritization slows the game down by focusing on the right problems, and doing work that aligns with our purpose and goals. It gives you license to de-prioritize that which doesn't and justifiably defend that decision. Prioritization also enables and empowers your people and the work that they do. It gives them clarity to know that, above all else, these things will get done because they are directly aligned with our goals and purpose. When you and your team are hyper-focused on what is truly important, and there is firmness in your resolve to use your energy on those things, you empower your team to take control of their days and weeks. Suddenly things don't seem so overwhelming.

PLANNING

Assume a team or organization has defined their purpose and goals. With proper preparation, the team now has the basis upon which to create a plan, to define which activities support those goals.

Across all sports, the successful teams and players are those that have solid game plans. In football, for instance, the coaching staff will prepare by watching film of the opposing team and reviewing analytics to determine where they have advantages, or to spot tendencies on either side of the ball to exploit. From there, they'll determine which plays they'll likely run within certain packages or in certain situations to seize on those advantages or tendencies. Sometimes, an offensive coordinator will "script" the first ten or fifteen plays – not only to watch how the other team defends those plays (and if that's different than what showed up on film or analytics), but also to give the staff and players time to get a feel for the flow of the game and make more informed adjustments. Those adjustments will happen throughout the game.

> ### *Planning:*
> *Turning strategy into a known sequence, aligning actions, resources, and expectations before the moment demands them.*

It's not much different in business. Take annual planning. With purpose, goals and strategy in hand, a leader will document specific deliverables for the coming year. Then, she'll define what resources and dependencies are required for those deliverables to be met, identify potential roadblocks and set a target completion date for each in a manner that allows the team to reasonably complete each of them. Acknowledging that some of those roadblocks may happen, known or unknown, the leader will determine how she'll adjust the plan if necessary. This is where going back to the prioritization mindset will help. If she picked five major deliverables, and unplanned circumstances force her to cut it to four, she'll call out which one is going to be paused.

Just like the football coach, the business leader will make adjustments throughout the year. Having the "what ifs" mapped out in advance helps her communicate with her team.

Now she can provide clarity in the direction the team is going, her expectations of them, and have a good idea about potential adjustments. Her team leader will know, for instance, that a deadline he or she owns is coming in, say, six months. That team leader is aware of dependencies and other planned activities on the team's plate, and can work their way backward on the calendar to break the tasks down into reasonable blocks and timeframes. And carry that forward with his or her team. This significantly reduces the surprises, and accounts for them when they arise. And then the game slows down.

PRACTICE

Marquette basketball coach Al McGuire once jokingly said, "The best thing about freshmen is that they become sophomores." Long-time Virginia Tech defensive coordinator Bud Foster would often say of a young player, "He's getting used to a new terminology and scheme. His mind's tying up his feet a little bit." In each case, the coaches were talking about players for whom the game had not yet slowed down. The players needed experience. They needed reps. They needed to see and do, repeatedly and over time, in order for the play to be second nature to them.

They needed to practice.

Same goes for the frontline staff on your team. They need to see and do, repeatedly and over time, to become dependably proficient in their jobs. That repetition not only drives proficiency; it allows them to understand the nuances of their work in order to more easily spot anomalies and opportunities.

For leaders, there's no substitute for going through the experience of handling conflict, giving tough feedback or creating an annual strategy. I guarantee you'll be better at it on the twentieth time than you were the first.

Practice:

Reps with intention, creating growth through self-awareness and betterment. The more you do the right things the right way, the more second nature they become.

Whether it's processing a transaction, leading a large project or influencing others toward a strategic decision, you improve the more you do it. Malcom Gladwell said as much in his book, *Outliers*: "Practice isn't the thing you do once you're good. It's the thing you do that makes you good."

The time it takes to become proficient differs depending on role or subject matter, and some people naturally ascend more quickly. But in most meaningful situations, there's no substitute for having done it before. The more proficient your employees are, the more the work becomes second nature. Then your teams can more easily look peripherally, and spot opportunities and risks proactively. Waste in your processes that may have come from waiting for work to get done, or needing re-work, will decrease and you'll be a higher-performing team. The opportunities that come from leveraging prior experience to quickly make an informed strategic decision can be the difference between long-term success and failure.

BENEFITS OF SLOWING THE GAME DOWN

As a leader, slowing the game down doesn't guarantee success. It does, however, put you in a better position to succeed. Preparation, prioritization and planning calms down the noise. After years of practice, you begin to realize the compounding effect of all of those lessons. Fewer things surprise you. You're able to apply experiences of the past to the situation at hand, even if it's not the exact same situation. Even more powerful is that you're more equipped to look three or four steps ahead of an action or decision and realize the potential impact of your options. This ability to foresee potential challenges and opportunities allows you to proactively prepare and position your teams for success. Leaders who anticipate well are in a stronger position to make strategic decisions, adapt to new circumstances and thrive.

Ultimately, if you've built a team with folks who have a bias for action, high accountability and they've gotten reps (practice), then you instill the preparation, prioritization and planning, your team is going to be a leader in getting things done. This earns credibility, which can become a flywheel for further improvements. Sometimes, your team may feel like they're paying a "competency tax," where weaker organizations will not only defer to yours, but may offload work as well. I'd rather view "our reward for a good job is more work" as another opportunity to make a difference.

Another benefit to consistently getting things done? No one can deflect from the root cause of a problem by pointing out that your team isn't executing. Weak teams and people will do this from time to time. Rather than hit an issue head on, they may turn the debate into something else, thus perpetuating the problem. Deflection is the oxygen that fuels the problem, just like a fire. If you remove the possibility of this deflection, you can then place the focus squarely on solving it.

Now that we're slowing the game down, we're ready to explore the final two themes: **"Our Engagement"** and **"Find a Better Way."**

MAKE IT EASY, MAKE IT STICK

Most organizations are relationship-driven; consequently most problems are people problems. That's why **"Our Engagement"** is so important. Many people, teams and organizations fail to intentionally prioritize building and nurturing relationships. Relationships are how problems get solved, compromises are made, ideas are hatched. They are how things get done.

Connecting with anyone requires skills like empathy, candor, humility, and the art of asking good questions. But so often people will toil alone when together is better, leaving neither party in a stronger position and both the opportunity to assume negative intent.

In my career, I've found it's important that our business partners understand "why" and that risk management is as easy as possible. So, I dedicate a lot of effort to ensuring that programs, processes and behaviors are easy to understand and easy to do. In order to do that, I learned to listen more than I talk, which allows me to pick up on pain points or difficulties without assuming what they are, and to talk to them in their language.

Our Engagement

Our highest priority is to enable our business partners to effectively and efficiently manage their risk. In what ways should we strive to improve in this area?	
Guidepost	*"When you show deep empathy toward others, their defensive energy goes down, and positive energy replaces it. That's when you can get more creative in solving problems."* -Stephen Covey, Author/Speaker
Reflection Questions	• Do our business partners understand "why"? • Have we made risk management "as easy as possible" to do? • Do we know their pain points and are we actively helping to address them? • Have we defined our engagement models? How efficient and productive are they? • How can we positively influence activity planning and processes / systems that we do not own but are impacted by?

Figure 6-1

I also learned to change the way I speak to myself. Instead of assuming that the root cause of a disagreement, misunderstanding or failure lies somewhere else, I try to ask "What am I doing that's contributing to this problem?" In both cases, perfection isn't possible because I'm human, but practice makes closer-to-perfect.

I hope these behaviors set a good example and I do impress upon my team the importance of them. In the end, we want to be people that others *want* to work with, even when, especially when, things are difficult.

Finally, have we created the right models to improve our engagement? At one company, we were part of what can best be described as a many-to-many engagement model. Multiple policy-making teams with different expectations, priorities and perspectives were trying to communicate their expectations separately with over a dozen front-line businesses. Aside from the frustrating inconsistency in expectations, what was really maddening was the lack of coordinated planning, socialization and load balancing.

We built an engagement model that brought representatives of all groups together in a structured way on a consistent schedule. We set expectations on all parties involved. We created a venue to pressure test new or amended policies to ensure they were fit for purpose. Then, we established an approval and implementation mechanism that increased the ability of each group to amend their processes.

Making appearances in other team meetings is another, albeit narrower example. It allows you to be visible and human, to inform others of what you're working on and to let people connect with you. There has to be purpose behind each appearance. While giving regular progress updates to leaders and teams in your environment is great, it's only important to the recipients if they know how that progress impacts them. When you've proven that you're getting things done and making their lives easier, the door can start to swing both ways.

FIND A BETTER WAY

It's easy for employees to get caught up in the never-ending cycle of corporate management. It's also easy for them to lose motivation due to whatever happens to be important this year amid deadlines, reductions in staff, cost constraints and the like.

In my world, some risk professionals struggle to stay motivated by good risk management practices, especially the younger ones. "You mean, if we do our job right, nothing happens?" was the vibe I got. One motivator that energizes most people, however, is making things better. Connecting the work that we do to a higher purpose allows us to be inspired and fulfilled, with a greater opportunity to innovate.

Complexity isn't typically efficient, nor is it scalable. It's also frustrating when it's avoidable, and often requires heroism, which isn't sustainable, in order to succeed. Give people the ability to call it by name and empower them to eradicate it, and watch engagement soar. When employed well, a continuous improvement mindset becomes a self-perpetuating, motivating culture. It rewards the naturally curious, emboldens those with a bias for action and it brings together those that trust, that are curious, that are not judgmental.

Relieving the team from the burden that is perfection is a necessary cultural mindset shift as well, because it allows for progress. As Mark Twain once said, "continuous improvement is better than delayed perfection."

Find a Better Way

There is always a better way, and it's our responsibility to find it.	
Guidepost	*"The thing is, continuity of strategic direction and continuous improvement in how you do things are absolutely consistent with each other. In fact, they're mutually reinforcing."* *-Michael Porter, Economist/Author*
Reflection Questions	• Does _____ help our business partners manage their risk, or does it add unnecessary complexity? • Do we care about the artifact, or the use of it (form vs substance)? • Opportunities are present everywhere we look; are we conditioned to look? • Are we preparing, prioritizing and planning sufficiently enough to slow the game down? • What are we doing well (keep)? What are we doing poorly (improve)? What can we stop doing (stop)?

Figure 6-2

Marv Adams, who I mentioned earlier in the book, was a champion of lean management systems and brought them to the company where we both worked. In an interview with McKinsey & Company's "The Lean Management Enterprise" magazine, Marv espoused the benefit of focusing on end-to-end processes from the client's perspective, and ignoring the boundaries between teams. By doing this, opportunities to improve start to appear, and the organization shifts to collaborating across teams and solving problems together. Marv perfectly encapsulated the benefits:

> *As a result, the organization begins to simplify itself. Left on its own, almost any organization evolves in a way that*

> *leads to what I call "valueless complexity." People assume that things are done in a certain way because that is the way they need to be done. Very often, however, what has actually happened is that a practice developed for a very specific time and purpose has crept into processes that it was never intended for. And in larger organizations, these intrusions proliferate to become bureaucracy.*
>
> *Much of the time, associates can see the problem, but they feel powerless to make changes. Lean management gives them the voice, structure, and tools to challenge long-standing assumptions—and the freedom to question how the organization does certain things and why. The effect is to help simplify and root out valueless complexity every day at the working level of the organization.*

The opportunities to drive out valueless complexity and suboptimal activities are everywhere. Our duty as leaders is to urge people to look for them and call them out, then empower them to eradicate them. There are plenty of tools in the lean management toolkit to help with this, some of which may be relevant to your business than others; whatever you implement, you have to instill and perpetuate the proper mindset. Make it exciting, even fun, for people to tap into their curiosity. Make it liberating to ask why we do something a certain way, or at all.

Atop every white board in every office I occupied for the past decade plus was the phrase "How did you get better today?" It always served as a personal reminder, but it was intentionally visible to others.

Reflection Prompts

- When does my team most often feel "scrambled" or reactive, and what's the root cause?
- When was the last time I personally modeled preparation that changed the trajectory of a decision or meeting?
- What recurring process feels more complicated than it should? What value is it actually delivering?
- How well do I help my team connect their daily work to our larger purpose?
- Where am I over-engineering something that could be simpler?

Intentional Actions

- Set aside 15 minutes each week to identify one process, meeting, or report to eliminate, simplify, or automate.
- Review your team's work-in-progress list and identify which items directly support purpose-aligned outcomes, and which don't.
- Ask 2-3 cross-functional partners this week what's hard about working with your team, and what would make things easier.
- Add "How did you get better today?" to your team's daily or weekly standups.

Closing Thoughts:

If Part I of this book was about the inner work that grounds us (clarifying who we are, what we're for, and how we show up), then Part II has been about putting that work into motion, and building something real with it.

Having a culture that aligns with your purpose and drives high performance doesn't magically happen. It's built intentionally. And success isn't just about having a vision; it's about building teams, systems, and structures that can bring that vision to life.

These past three chapters weren't written as a playbook, but as a lived experience. I didn't get these things right from day one. I learned, often the hard way, that transactional leadership gets transactional results. I had to evolve from a mindset of "execution first" to one of "alignment first." That shift changed everything, but I'm still learning every day.

We covered a lot. The anatomy of a high-performing team. The importance of hiring and growing people who align with your values. The impact of clarity, and why it's not just helpful, but non-negotiable. The structural work of building systems, rituals and rhythms that make culture visible and repeatable. The mindset shift from "just get it done" to "get it done right, together, for a purpose."

We also spent time on the disciplines that help slow the game down: preparation, prioritization, planning, and practice. They're the difference between leading from calm or chaos, intention or instinct.

We wrapped with engagement and continuous improvement. In my world, those two are everything. Relationships are how things get done. "Finding a better way" is what keeps things moving forward and people motivated. Even when the work is hard, even when the world around us isn't cooperating.

We've explored what it means to lead ourselves. We've seen how to build aligned cultures and purposeful organizations. In the final section that follows, we'll focus on sustaining it. Leadership is never a one-and-done exercise. It's a constant rhythm of reflection, connection, continuous improvement and legacy. These final chapters explore the habits, practices, and personal motivations that bring it all to life, and to sustain it, even after you're gone.

For now, though, I'd leave you with this:

You won't see a thriving culture in a slide deck. You'll see it in how you hire, how you interact, how you follow up. You'll see it in how decisions are made, and who gets to make them. You'll see it in how problems are solved, and who feels safe enough to point them out. You'll see it in what you tolerate, and what you don't.

High-performing teams don't just work harder. They work smarter, with trust as the default and purpose as the compass.

And leadership? Real leadership is making it easier for your team to do the right thing, the right way, for the right reasons…without having to ask.

PART III: THE ENDURING WORK

Practices that Drive Results and Meaning

Chapter 7:

Swallow Hard and Lead

Bo Pelini had an opportunity, and he squandered it.

Pelini was relieved of his duties as the head coach of the Nebraska Cornhuskers football team on November 30, 2014 after the final game of a 9-3 season. Throughout and after his tenure, the emotional coach retained a large number of supporters. His dismissal was quite the story on the local and national level.

By many measures, Pelini was a successful college head football coach. During his seven years in Lincoln, only Alabama's Nick Saban won more games. It was hard to argue with his talent on the sidelines. This, however, is a story about leadership in tough moments.

Two days after he was let go, Pelini surreptitiously gathered his players at a local high school in Lincoln for a final farewell meeting.

This was his opportunity.

Pelini had a captive audience of young men, aged 18-22, who followed him into battle every Saturday. For many, he was a father figure. For some, he was their only father figure.

He took the spotlight one final time as this impressionable group's leader. When I heard about this meeting, I was glad that he and his team had this opportunity for closure and hopeful that the coach would gracefully share one final lesson. After all, there have been many examples of coaches who left their teams without so much as a goodbye.

Two weeks after the meeting, though, an audio tape of it leaked, and it certainly wasn't what I had hoped for. His remarks to the team were heavy on foul language and light on emotional maturity.

Pelini had an opportunity to show his team how to handle adversity. He had an opportunity to tell his players that the institution where he recruited them to get their education and play football was, indeed, still the first class place he said it was when they were high-schoolers. He had an opportunity to acknowledge that maybe, just maybe, he bore some responsibility for his fate. And he had an opportunity to tell them one last time how much he cared for them.

On all but the last, he failed quite spectacularly.

Pelini used this opportunity to blame others completely for his dismissal. He disparaged those people with deeply inappropriate vulgarities. He showed zero respect for others' viewpoints, as well as for the University of Nebraska, which incidentally would still be home for most of his players after he left town. Good luck, boys, this place is a disaster!

Whether or not Pelini's opinions were valid was not the issue. He squandered an opportunity to teach his team that sometimes things don't go your way, and you need to handle it with class.

He could have proven that humility and grace are character traits you should anchor to. Instead, by his actions, he modeled that it's okay to shift blame rather than take responsibility…at exactly the moment when grace was most needed.

Whether or not his words should have been recorded or leaked also wasn't the point. That he said those words at all, frankly, was.

It is often said that you find out more about someone's character in tough times than you do in good times. This, unfortunately, was a case study in just that.

Especially in times of adversity, you have a leadership opportunity. These are the times when others who follow you are more acutely aware of your words and actions. These may be the times when you don't *want* to lead with grace, patience, humility, but they're when it matters the most. This is a chapter about emotional intelligence.

EMOTIONAL INTELLIGENCE 101

Daniel Goleman is a world-renowned psychologist and author, known to many for his book *Emotional Intelligence* in 1995 and considerable companion and follow-on work in this space in the years since.

For most of the 20th century, we looked to the Intelligence Quotient (IQ) as the barometer for intelligence and harbinger for success. Goleman's core assertions were that while both IQ and emotional intelligence are important for developing into a good leader, leaders who have high emotional intelligence are more effective and achieve greater long-term success than those who do not. He also noted that the way the brain develops means that as humans mature and add experience, their emotional intelligence can grow over time.

Over the years, Goleman's presentation of emotional intelligence components have evolved to four main areas.

Self-Awareness focuses on understanding our own emotions, strengths, weaknesses, values and motivations. It's knowing who we are and why. Self-awareness means noticing how you show up, how others are reacting to you, and being able to *diagnose your own impact* in real time and after the fact. We covered this topic extensively in Chapter 1.

Self-Management goes beyond understanding who we are and how we act and centers on our ability to manage all of that. Having emotional self-control, an ability to adapt to change, being goal-oriented and generally having an optimistic outlook are indicators of this domain. This may show up in your ability to pause before you speak, or maybe when you shift tactics in a meeting because the situation calls for a different approach.

Social Awareness is essentially about understanding the emotions and perspectives of others. Having empathy, an understanding of the organization around you and an ability to read the room, and other people, are the hallmarks here. Do you know the power structures in your company? Do you know how work gets done, or which people and groups work well together, or potentially can? Who do you need to better understand? Not to win an argument necessarily, but to align with your shared goals.

Lastly, **Relationship Management** seems fairly self-explanatory, but there are a multitude of competencies in play here. Among them are influencing others, managing conflict, inspiring others, mentoring and finding common ground to facilitate teamwork. Where the first three domains are either introspective or otherwise focused on self, this domain is where you tap into your ability to impact what other people do. This is where you build trust, resolve tension, foster collaboration and influence others to move forward for a common goal or purpose.

BRINGING IT TO LIFE

Coach Pelini's example shows that, while he was a good "X's and O's" coach and effective leader of young men in some respects, he probably didn't get a passing grade in any of these emotional intelligence domains.

The best thing about experiences and missteps, our own or others', is that we can learn from them. As Goleman asserts, because we can develop in these domains, we can apply those learnings to support our own growth.

Because good examples of emotional intelligence at work are not typically comprised of a one-competency silo, I like to think of situations that employ two or more domains and competencies to bring it to life.

For example, we once had an initiative that required work from three teams, one of which sat in my organization. The leader on my team had all of the relevant knowledge and risk chops necessary to speak on our behalf, certainly more than me. However, the other two teams were looking to me as a decision maker necessary to keeping the initiative moving. I quickly realized I could take a back seat to the leader on my team. I positioned her as my proxy with the others, which removed a bottleneck and increased speed to completion. It benefited me because I could spend my time more wisely. It benefited her too because it tapped into her abilities and established her as a leader in that space.

In this example, I was pairing adaptability (a competency under Self-Management) with teamwork (Relationship Management). Doing so properly helped me understand that adapting role structure was entirely appropriate given the situation to ease a logjam and to act more quickly.

And there were, of course, short- and long-term benefits to this intentional action. My adaptability promoted the ownership of ideas on my team rather than rigid deference, fostering growth. More importantly, it legitimized someone else's perspectives in others' eyes. This was appropriate because she had more subject matter expertise and was closer to the problem, boosting our team's value.

Leading up to that moment, I had taken the time to understand the depth of knowledge of this team leader, as well as gauge her emotional intelligence. Over the course of multiple conversations, I'd ask, "What do you think?" and then shut up for a while. It was clear she knew what she was talking about. I found her thought process on track, and her communication articulate. So, I was comfortable enough to let my opinions take a back seat and move to more of a support role.

Had I not recognized the situation or chose not to be as adaptable, perhaps the initiative would have still been completed on time.

But at what cost?

There would have been more bottlenecks because of me, and probably some last-minute fire drills. I would have spent more time on that initiative than I should, compromising my ability to give proper attention to other work that aligned with our goals and purpose. Perhaps most damaging, though, would have been the lost opportunity for a key leader on my team to grow.

MODELING EMOTIONAL INTELLIGENCE

As a leader, it's important to remember that emotional intelligence doesn't stay confined to you. It spreads. Whether you intend to or not, you set the tone for your team. If you're calm, open, and self-aware, others are more likely to be. If you're reactive or inconsistent, they'll mirror that too.

In addition to your team tending to take on your characteristics, there's a subtle yet positive impact made on your team when they generally know how you will act or react. That's not to say that you will always behave the same way. Of course, certain situations may call for a different tactic. In those cases, when appropriate, you can explicitly tell your team why you acted differently than they may have expected.

Understanding that emotional intelligence, yours and your team's, is a dynamic component to the culture that you're building and nurturing, it's important to spend energy on its development. Here are a few practical ways to model and coach emotional intelligence.

Normalize Feedback Loops: Make reflection part of the rhythm of your team, as a normal post-mortem and not just when something goes wrong. This can be done with a key person on your team or in small groups. Perhaps have a debrief after a particularly notable meeting, and ask questions like:

- What felt right about that meeting, and what felt off?
- Where did that conversation turn in a way we didn't expect?
- How might we start that meeting differently next time?

When you ask these questions as a leader, and answer them yourself, you teach your team that emotional self-assessment is not just okay, it's expected. It emphasizes the virtue of self-awareness, psychological safety and learning agility.

Reward Calm Under Pressure: In high-stress moments, what you reward becomes the bar. It's easy to reward speed or boldness, but take note when someone slows things down thoughtfully or keeps the team steady in tension. Publicly call out the behavior: "You stayed level-headed during that escalation. That kind of presence lowers the temperature and it builds trust." This establishes a real-world example for others to follow. When they see that it happened, that it worked, and that you noticed, it'll be easier for the next person to take that step forward.

Debrief Emotional Moments Openly: After a tough conversation, a major pivot, or an unexpected conflict, come back to a key member of your team to debrief. Not just for strategy, but for a check-in on the emotional part of it.

For instance, ask, *"How did that land with you?"* or *"That was an important moment. Are you good with where we ended up?"* Be willing to go first with your own vulnerability. Be willing to listen. The goal is to show that emotional responses are not signs of weakness, they're data points. If appropriate, use the time to provide context or reasoning behind your approach to that conversation. Depending on the situation, it may be best to give the moment some time to breathe before having a debrief.

WHEN IT'S HARD (BECAUSE IT WILL BE)

Emotional intelligence isn't a tool for when things are going smoothly. In fact, it reveals itself most clearly, and develops more quickly, when things are messy, tense, or personal. That's why I chose *Swallow Hard and Lead* for the chapter title.

It's easy to be composed when no one's pushing your buttons. It's a lot harder when you're blindsided in a meeting, when someone disappoints you, when your ego is bruised or you're under stress. That's when emotional intelligence becomes real. It's not about being perfectly calm; rather, it's about being aware enough to know what's happening inside you, and intentional enough not to be controlled by it. That's when you have the opportunity not just to navigate the challenge, but to thrive in it. To take advantage of the moment in a way that creates a win and changes the trajectory of your organization.

Self-awareness under pressure is a different muscle than self-awareness during reflection.

Do you ever see an email chain as if it was a car wreck in slow motion? One snarky reply-all followed by a passive-aggressive response? And besides asking yourself why you're even on the cc: line, you wonder *"why don't they just pick up the phone?"*

I worked with a gentleman 10 or 15 years ago – a good man who, unfortunately, just couldn't control his anger. His release was to fire off an email to whomever was the target of his ire, warranted or not. Sometimes, the recipient would temporarily diffuse it; other times, it escalated…quickly. If I happened to be on the thread and saw the regrettable discourse first hand, I would pop up and take a stroll down to this person's office. We had developed a good rapport; he didn't feel threatened by me, and I feel like he trusted my intentions. I'd ask him what all the fuss was about and let him explain it to me face-to-face. Typically, even if he was still angry about whatever it was, you could see his temperature drop just by spending a few minutes talking to a human being about it. Maybe it was because I was a third party, or because it was a conversation instead of an email, but it usually worked.

I'm certain that I've sent emails that I shouldn't have. Seeing instances like this play out, however, made me much more aware of how I was communicating. The impact of what we say and do can be long-lasting and far-reaching, even more so what we write. My draft folder is a graveyard of emails I never intend to send. Sometimes, it's good to put our feelings down, then pause to consider the future impacts of our next action. More often, then, we ultimately say the right thing, with the right tone, to get to the right outcome.

Not only will you solve problems and address conflict more proficiently, you'll offer an example for others in your circle of influence to follow. You show them that you are the person you would want others to be. You show them that you treat others how you would want to be treated. You show them grace and maturity.

Reflection Prompts

- When have I "swallowed hard and led"? What did I learn about myself, and what did others see in that moment?
- What do I tend to do when I feel frustrated, blindsided, or under pressure, and how does that impact others?
- How do I show emotional transparency with my team? Do they understand my intentions when the stakes are high?
- What's one relationship I'm managing today that would benefit from greater empathy or curiosity?

Intentional Actions

- The next time you're tempted to fire off a reactive email, draft it, but don't send it for 24 hours. Revisit with clarity the next day.
- After a difficult meeting or conflict, schedule 10 minutes with a trusted peer to debrief emotionally, not just tactically.
- Choose a moment in the next week to explain the strategic reasoning behind a leadership choice you made
- Ask someone on your team: "What's something that's been weighing on you that I might not be seeing?"
- For one week, scan your sent emails for tone and emotional clarity. Ask yourself: "Would I want to be on the receiving end of this?"

Chapter 8:

Before You Give Advice...

I don't recall the most meaningful conversations in my career coming with a label. I rarely heard, "Hey, let me coach you for a few minutes" or "Time for a feedback session." But there they were, and it was these moments that helped me level up, personally and professionally. Sometimes, the impact was immediate; others set me on a different path to self-improvement. I think about Steve Beck's story in Chapter 1, and how it redirected my whole trajectory. Or the way Marv Adams modeled intentional leadership without ever needing to say that's what he was doing.

As I grew in my own career, I began to realize how much of leadership is about shaping people. And the tools we have to do that aren't generally grand strategies or annual plans. In fact, if the only time you engage with others about how they're doing, what they're doing and how they're doing it is during annual performance reviews, you're missing the boat. No, often, the moments are smaller and more human: a question well-asked, a perspective offered at the right time, a challenge with care and intention behind it. Or just listening. In this chapter, let's unpack three of the most powerful tools we have to shape others - mentoring, coaching, and feedback – and how I've come to use and evolve them over the years.

MENTORING: SHARE YOUR PATH TO ILLUMINATE THEIRS

I like to think of mentoring as legacy work. It's long-view and relationship-based, and its purpose is rooted in guidance and exposure. It happens when someone with experience (mentor) provides support for the growth, both personal and professional, of another person (mentee). Mentoring activities can be episodic, but the relationships are typically long-term, often lasting many years.

Mentoring should happen naturally with anyone in your direct sphere of accountability, and the amount of time you invest in someone should be directly correlated with how he or she scores on the "Build Around Those…" model from Chapter 4.

It can also happen formally or informally in an organization that supports a mentor program, or when would-be mentees seek it out. I can't recall ever turning down a request to mentor someone, and considered it an honor and a duty to do so if someone took the initiative to ask.

Both parties have a responsibility in a mentoring relationship, particularly in preparation, attention and thoughtfulness. The mentee should be clear with themselves and the mentor what their goal is for the relationship and to follow through on that. The mentor, in particular, should lead with curiosity, avoid judgment, and skew towards sharing experiences rather than dictating next steps.

Mostly, the mentor should feel obligated to listen first.

Some of the greatest compliments I've gotten have been from leaders on my team who thanked me for simply listening to them. Not trying to solve their problems, but letting them talk them out, and guiding them along the path to solution.

And both parties stand to benefit from it. For the mentee, it's a safe space to "test out" their ideas, approach or assessment of a situation, and have them validated or nudged slightly. It aids in their emotional intelligence journey and can even help expand their network. For the mentor, it's a chance to get out of their own bubble and hear the perspective of someone who sits in a different seat, and perhaps a different generation. By sharing their experiences, it may stoke their own personal reflection. And, frankly, it just feels rewarding to help someone else.

David Kimm, who I mentioned in Chapter 3, was always willing to hear what I had to say and thoughtfully answer my questions in our dozen years of working together. We might set aside time for a breakfast or lunch meeting, or it might be a phone call or a drop-in to his office. It was a chance for us to share perspectives on current happenings in our programs and at our company. More so, it was my chance to ask David how he approached handling conflict or diffusing caustic situations, or how he explained risk management to those struggling to understand it.

From our earliest time working together, David saw in me someone worth investing in, even if I had a lot of growing to do. It's no coincidence that a big part of my growth happened during this time. It led to him pushing me out of my comfort zone and sponsoring me for stretch assignments. I also knew I could be direct with David without reluctance because it was a relationship built on trust, something that benefited him as well.

COACHING: HELP THEM SEE AND GROW

Where mentoring may be longer-form and development-driven, coaching is more performance-based, often time-bound and focused on attaining specific tangible goals or honing a skill or competency. This can run the gamut from ascending the learning curve of a job to leading a project to being a stronger public speaker or influencer.

A coaching relationship may be more structured and potentially more directive than mentoring. Like a mentor, the ideal outcomes typically happen when the coach listens and asks good questions. There are a couple of reasons for this.

First, in our zeal to "fix" whatever is not working, and often pressed for time, we have a tendency to jump to the solution as quickly as possible. As a coach, intentional listening coupled with questions like *"What does a positive outcome here look like for you?"* or *"What specifically do you need from me?"* can give you clarity on the situation and what role you should play.

Second, the best coaches are not the ones who give the answer to the question but the ones who walk the person they're coaching down the path to the right answer. It's through thoughtful questions that we accomplish that. Asking "What do you see as your obstacles to getting this done?" or "What, in your mind, is the most important thing to focus on?" give both of you an opportunity. For the person being coached, it's an opportunity to try out their idea with some guardrails prior to acting. For the coach, it's an opportunity to assess the other person's mastery and, of course, to properly be the guardrail.

Very early in my career, as I was learning the ins and outs of brokerage operations and credit/margin operations in particular, I had a team leader named Gray Houghton. Gray was friendly, firm when he needed to be and someone I really enjoyed working with. He was also a wise-cracker who kept things light on the floor with dry wit and humor, equally at ease taking jabs as he was giving them. Above it all, he was very good at his job and willing to share his knowledge with newbies.

I will forever be grateful for how Gray handled my litany of questions. What's unique about Gray is that, throughout our time working together, I don't ever remember him answering my questions with a direct answer. He typically chose one of two responses.

If he assessed that this was a teaching moment, he would start with explaining the situation at hand, where it fit contextually within the bigger picture, what the appropriate answer or course of action was – and why.

If he assessed that I had the answer inside of me, he'd lean back, look me in the eye and say, "What do you think the answer is?" and the conversation would go from there. Either way, the result was that I got better, and I did so much more quickly and sustainably.

Thank you, Gray.

FEEDBACK: TO BE DIRECT IS TO BE KIND

Feedback is giving someone information from your perspective in order to promote improvement and continued development. It can be positive or negative, but must be constructive to reach its desired result. It is a technique that can be used as part of structured formats, like during a performance review or as part of a mentoring or coaching relationship. It can also be used in informal, episodic ways. What's unique about feedback is that it's delivered because the person giving it has observed an action, behavior, competency or trait and wants to use that observation as an opportunity to help the person receiving it improve.

I've given and received feedback hundreds of times in my career. In my opinion, its impact is positively correlated with three features:

- the respect each party has for one another

- the trust in the relationship
- the way it is delivered

Think about it.

If you respect my opinion, we have built a foundation of trust and I deliver feedback in a way that is constructive, thoughtful and direct, why *wouldn't* you appreciate hearing it? Conversely, it might be really hard for you to hear what I had to say if those one or two of those weren't present.

In an established mentoring or coaching relationship where trust and respect are cemented, maybe the delivery becomes slightly less important. But when they're not cemented, or when the feedback is unsolicited, the more thoughtfulness and constructiveness become prerequisites.

There was a very talented direct report on my team once. She had deep knowledge, was a phenomenal operator and she got things done. High accountability, with a skill set complementary to mine. Just a joy to work with. We had developed a strong and trusted relationship over the years that organically and unofficially branched into mentoring and coaching as well. We didn't have to worry what the motives were for what one another said, and we easily assumed positive intent.

One area of growth opportunity for her was speaking with executives – clear articulation of the situation and proposed solution, buoyed by pertinent facts with the ability to delve into details as necessary, stopping to listen to what the executive had to say, not interrupting. After one meeting with another executive, she asked me how I thought it went. I told her, "*You covered everything you needed to, and we'll get there, but next time you'll want to get to the punch line more quickly, and let the executive speak. If you want to practice, let me know.*" She had told me that this wasn't the first time she'd gotten that feedback, and was really interested in addressing it.

She improved considerably after that conversation in just a short amount of time. My feedback in and of itself wasn't outstanding, but we certainly had a solid relationship built on trust. In the past, perhaps she wasn't yet ready to intentionally improve in this area. Or maybe the previous feedback didn't land because the trust, respect or delivery wasn't there.

A comment on directness: being direct, to me, is an act of kindness. You care enough about a person that you're not going to beat around the bush. But being direct will not be effective without those three things (respect, trust, delivery). I've gotten lots of "direct" feedback over the years from people that I didn't trust or didn't respect or who delivered it in a non-constructive manner. "Telling it like it is" is not a license to say whatever you want if you want it to be effective.

When you deliver it in a way that people can reasonably accept it's coming from the right place, being direct is the best way.

I mentioned feedback can be both positive and negative. If the only time you give feedback is when it's negative, you've missed out on the opportunity to help another person grow and your relationship to grow. "That was fantastic! Do more of that!" is great feedback when it's warranted. Mix in some positive reinforcement along the way; it can be just as helpful as constructive, negative feedback and the two combined will make both more impactful.

Mentoring, coaching, and feedback are tools that can benefit both others and ourselves, when used with care and consistency. They don't require special titles, formal structures, or longwinded performance decks. What they do require is presence, trust, and the courage to speak with honesty and humility. Whether it's a one-off moment in a hallway or a standing conversation over years, the influence we have on others is often forged in these intentional exchanges. So don't wait for the perfect moment. Start where you are, with what you know, and with whom you're already leading. This is how we grow. This is how we lead better.

Reflection Prompts

- When have I received mentoring, coaching, or feedback that changed my trajectory? What made it stick?
- Where might someone on my team need support, but hasn't asked?
- Are my one-on-one meetings focused only on tasks, or am I also helping people grow?
- What does my approach to developing others say about my leadership legacy?

Intentional Actions

- Identify one person in your organization you believe in, reach out this week and offer yourself as a mentor or sounding board.
- Before your next feedback conversation, write down one question that will help the other person reflect before you offer advice.
- In your next discussion with a mentee, write down a few open-ended questions that allow them to do most of the talking, and you to primarily listen.

Chapter 9:

Time to Think

It was March 4, 1993 and Jim Valvano was dying of cancer. The 47-year-old former NC State basketball coach, most famous at that point for his team's improbable National Championship a decade earlier, was now feebly making his way to the stage of the ESPY Awards to become most famous for something else:

> *"To me, there are three things we all should do every day. We should do this every day of our lives. Number one is laugh. You should laugh every day. Number two is think. You should spend some time in thought. Number three is you should have your emotions moved to tears, could be happiness or joy. But think about it. If you laugh, you think and you cry, that's a full day. That's a heck of a day. You do that seven days a week, you're going to have something special."*

This was a man less than eight weeks away from death sharing wisdom and unveiling the motto, "Don't Give Up, …Don't Ever Give Up" in the fight against cancer to a worldwide audience. I've thought of that speech and these words often since then. I can only imagine the gravity of the thoughts in a person's head when he or she has some certainty about how much time is left. Recently, I've become more focused on the concepts of time and thinking.

Time is an interesting phenomenon. When you're young, it's an infinite and unimportant commodity. As you get older, how you spend it has a way of becoming considerably more important - more so than the things that were important back in the day. Tomorrow is promised to no one, so why not be more intentional about how we spend our time.

Whether or not we use it wisely in our work life is a big driver in how successful we and our teams are. Take meetings, for example. A study by Atlassian revealed that the average professional spends 31 hours per month, and U.S. businesses waste about $37 billion dollars per year, in unproductive meetings. You could blame poor meeting structure as a culprit and you wouldn't be wrong. Still, it is people who convene meetings. Do people prioritize thinking, for themselves and others? Do they create the right environments to productively think?

Thinking. It seems that heeding the advice to think has become increasingly hard for us. Most people don't have the time, or don't make the time to do it anymore. Or they forgot how to.

Yes, we "think" every day. We process information. We make decisions. But how often do we truly spend time *in thought?* And is it enough?

A SHRINKING ATTENTION SPAN

It appears that the average American's attention span has dwindled to microscopic levels. While this aided in sparking the Information Age, it also became a symptom of it.

Cable television turned the 6 o'clock news hour into a 24/7 affair, which led to having to fill 24 hours with content, any content. Then came the internet. Then Google. Then social media. Now AI. That there is a ubiquitous initialism (TL;DR) to tell others an article, email or story is too long to take time to read speaks volumes about where we are today.

Gone are the days when we got our information at appointed times (e.g. morning paper, evening news). In those days we digested it, formulated an opinion and talked about it.

Then we sat down and read a book.

According to Pew Research, 77% of Americans in 2020 read at least one book during the previous year, down from 92% in 1978. What is everyone doing with their time? Well, 73% of Americans currently use at least one form of social media. That's up from 0% in 1978, of course.

THE COST OF NOISE

We have so much information at our fingertips now. It is powerful and efficient, to be sure. It also comes with an unintended consequence: the time that we used to spend thinking is now interrupted by our phone buzzing with another text, tweet, Facebook update, snapchat…

A study by MNTN Research revealed that up to 83% of our country watches a second device while also watching TV. I'm guilty of it. Statistically speaking, you're likely just as guilty.

All of this has changed the way that companies try to sell us their products. It's changed how politicians campaign and govern, and how the media cover them. From companies and politicians to influencers and thought leaders, anyone with a product, service or opinion to sell now competes to be the loudest or the most sensational – because their consumers only have a few seconds until it's on to the next piece of "BREAKING NEWS".

It feels like political debates used to have more meaningful dialogue about substantive matters. At least they were graded based on who outperformed the other. Now debates are graded based on who delivered the best one-liner. And there are hundreds of media outlets spending endless 24-hour cycles as information Pez dispensers, telling us what we should think in incessant, easily-digestible doses.

At work, we are constantly called upon to help solve problems or give our time to others' priorities. We have demanding calendars that, if we're being honest, contain plenty of meetings that don't require our presence. We get hundreds of emails, phone calls and instant messages every day.

The din has never been louder.

Strategic thinking isn't just about planning big moves. It's about becoming the kind of leader who doesn't react on instinct alone. In a world where immediacy is mistaken for effectiveness, the leaders who create space to breathe, notice, and course-correct are the ones who make better decisions and build better teams. So, what are we to do?

TAKE TIME TO THINK

Given the choice, I believe we'd all prefer to be more thoughtful, and to be considered as such. Certainly, we would opt for contemplative and reflective over shallow and flippant. We'd be more comfortable about our decisions if we took the opportunity to discern potential impacts or consequences before moving, thoughtfully, and with regard for others.

How often do we study an issue from all sides? Or ask people who know more about something than we do what they think? Do we take time to understand differing viewpoints? Do we do it more or less often than we did ten years ago? It takes more effort today than it did when Coach Valvano spoke over 30 years ago, but it's doable.

It's also necessary.

In strategic work, reclaiming time to reflect, recalibrate, and refocus is vital because strategy needs space to breathe. Just as we're becoming wired to quickly gather information, we're wired to quickly act based on it. Constant motion dilutes quality thinking and often yields to tactical, reactive leadership. Taking a purposeful Strategic Pause isn't avoidance of action; instead, it creates the foundation to act wisely.

Let's break Strategic Pause into three types:

Personal pause is intentional space to reflect - weekly, monthly, or life-stage. Socrates famously said, "The only true wisdom is in knowing you know nothing." Accepting your small place in this world and realizing how little you know takes some humility. Once you do that, though, the door opens and you're free to think and learn as much as you want. If humility is the door, prioritizing it in your life is choosing to walk through the doorway.

Some people like to think during early morning meditation or exercise. Some take to journaling. Still others schedule it into their calendar and (hopefully) don't schedule over it. Even something as simple as regular rituals to prompt you to think, such as my whiteboard question "How did you get better today?" might work. Personal pause isn't indulgent, and it's certainly not frivolous. It's an investment in yourself and ultimately your strategic edge.

By the way, a byproduct of personal pause, in my opinion, is gratitude. These moments have a way of helping you reflect on those who have helped your cause or lit the way for you. Showing gratitude seems more and more like a lost art and that makes me sad. The emergence of email and text messaging hasn't helped matters, but they are not the root cause. I think it's often because we don't take the time to reflect on what, and who, we're grateful for. The importance of this simple act cannot be understated. Think about how good you felt the last time someone expressed sincere appreciation to you. Use personal pause to find gratitude, and pay it forward.

Team pause is stepping back to ask "What are we doing, and why?" There is a time and a place for this type of pause, and it's not in a regular weekly leadership huddle. It requires the right brain space and the right environment for this type of pause to be successful. That environment requires the part of the brain that is not wired for action, but for contemplation.

In Nancy Kline's insightful book *Time to Think*, she delves into the ten components of "The Thinking Environment" that allow us to set the right conditions for quality thought. This can be something as simple as a physically comfortable room free of distractions, or as complex as our conscious and unconscious behavior in that room.

For instance, have you ever observed someone who was listening to *respond* rather than listening to *understand*? How much thought is happening in that person's head? How much thinking is happening in a room that becomes a speaking contest? In her book, Ms. Kline discusses the importance of mutual agreement of interest. When we can agree to be interested in what each other has to say, and genuinely interested in where the other person will go next in their thinking, then we become almost averse to interrupting. We've leaned in. There's no need for me to interrupt if I'm fascinated by where you might go next. Now you have a room where people are silent but actively listening, and the room becomes more thoughtful as a result.

A team pause will help you pull people above the fray and ask, "Is this still the right way to go?" or "Where are our activities out of alignment with our purpose and goals?" And with the right environment, you and your leaders and colleagues can more astutely ascertain future actions.

Organizational pause can be found in moments of reevaluation. Organizations need moments to catch their breath. It's not too dissimilar to team pause in terms of conditions for success, but is marked by circumstances that require consideration of longer-term changes in trajectory or approach. The inflection points that dictate a need for organizational pause may be leadership change (yours or above you), restructures or acquisitions, fiscal year planning or post-crisis recovery. Organizational pause flies at a higher altitude than other pauses, and the resulting actions peer over a longer horizon.

The cultural concepts that I employ (Anatomy of a Successful Team, Cultural Themes, etc.) that we covered in Part II? It is in sessions featuring organizational pause that I introduce and revisit them. The concepts, guideposts and reflection questions were written precisely to benefit from organizational pause. These are the sessions where I listen to my leadership team's thoughts on how we should - and do - operationalize those cultural themes and leverage the feedback into actions going forward.

The overriding themes here are intentional in nature; intentionally creating the right environment for deeper thought and intentionally prioritizing it in the first place. The noise that comes from everyone and everywhere else demanding your attention won't be quieted unless *you* quiet it. The finite amount of time you and your team have available won't make room for thought unless *you* make time for it.

So, make more time for it. Prioritize it. Set aside time for personal thought and reflection. Silence the phone. Start blocking off some time on your calendar, or better yet, do it early in the morning before anyone else is up. Declutter your mind. Choose a subject that matters, and commit time to think deeply, explore context and pursue quality insight. We need to prepare our mind in order to be less reactive. I know I can do more of this. Same goes for your teams. Their performance and engagement will improve in a thoughtful environment, and growth will follow. It will be another aid in slowing the game down, and it's time well spent. When we take time to think, as Coach Valvano said, we're going to have something special.

Reflection Prompts

- When was the last time I truly set aside time to think, without distraction?
- What are the recurring decisions or challenges I face that deserve deeper reflection?
- How does the current rhythm of my team support or hinder deep thinking and thoughtful discussion?
- What's one moment recently when I acted quickly but wished I'd paused first? What would I do differently next time?

Intentional Actions

- Block one hour per week in your calendar to step away and reflect on strategy or leadership.
- Schedule a team pause session each quarter to recalibrate goals, culture, and alignment. This shouldn't be extemporaneous, so set the expectation for pre-session thought.
- Send a short, preferably hand-written, note of gratitude to someone each week.
- Eliminate or rethink one recurring meeting that adds noise but no value, then reallocate that time to deeper work.

Chapter 10:

What's Most Important to You?

The steps we take through our lives and careers, all of the pivotal moments and experiences, shape our purpose. And that purpose can take root in multiple ways.

One way that I believe is imperative is to have a business-driven purpose. For me, no matter where I am or what role I'm filling, I always want to leave the organization and people I'm supporting better than I found them, and do so in a way that aligns with the company's purpose and strategy. This is important for obvious reasons, not least because the company that's hired you wants a return on its investment. It's also this purpose that, articulated clearly, forms the basis of your strategy and gives your organization something to connect to.

But I also believe that a career is more worthwhile and impactful when you can use it as a canvas to paint a picture of what's most important to you. To complete a journey that fulfills a personal purpose.

Mine begins here.

My mom's name is Anne Petera, and there is no one on this earth I am prouder of or look up to more. Her energy, work ethic and ability to relate to and influence others has had a big impact on me.

She got married and had me at a very early age. She put herself through night school for over six years when I was in elementary school to get her business degree. She worked full time throughout. Over the years she worked her way up, grew, remade herself numerous times, and ultimately served her state and her country with distinction in several capacities. Even with her ambitious schedule, she was a very supportive parent who never missed my little league games or other activities.

Mom and me after a little league football game, 1981

To say her career was remarkable doesn't do it justice, but in a career full of outstanding achievements, a big turning point early on led her to strive for more while reminding us of the struggles corporate America, and in particular financial services, has faced in diversity.

The first phase of my mom's career was in banking. She started out as a teller, then moved into gradually larger roles before learning a harsh reality of the era as it pertained to women in the industry.

The time period was the early 80's. Mom worked in Human Resources in a training and recruiting role, and had just received a promotion to an officer position in corporate finance, her dream destination. When she returned from her last campus recruiting trip, she was informed that the bank had rescinded her promotion and new job. The reason: the bank had eliminated the position of a man, and they wanted to find a position to put him in order to keep him. So they gave him hers. She was welcome to stay at the bank in her current role, of course. Of course…

She could have bemoaned her fate, or quietly accepted it. Instead, she used the episode as an opportunity. An opportunity to dictate for herself where her career went rather than rely on the whims of others.

That moment made my mom determined to prove to herself and perhaps others what she was capable of. She left the bank and immediately began a successful career in real estate, which gave her additional confidence. She parlayed years of volunteering and networking into multiple roles in state and federal government, including among them Secretary of the Commonwealth of Virginia and Assistant Secretary of Homeland Security.

Throughout her adult life, she never did anything halfway. She wasn't just a supportive little league parent – she wrote and submitted the articles for our games for our hometown newspaper. She wasn't just involved with her alma mater – she served as Vice Rector on its Board of Visitors. She didn't just go out and vote – she got involved in local politics and served her community. She didn't just sell real estate – she also became a real estate educator. As I said, she had (and still has) boundless energy, and made her own opportunities. But her experience at the bank – and how she was treated – was pivotal.

Our family with Secretary of Homeland Security Michael Chertoff after Mom's swearing in, 2007

While Mom's story is an interesting study in individual determination and making your own opportunities, I can't help but think about how far we've come from a diversity perspective in financial services – and how far we still have to go. I also wonder what her career in financial services would have looked like if she was treated appropriately.

Forty years ago, there was little or no support in the financial services industry for women and minorities. In an interview with the mentorship blog *j.jane*, my mom described the concept of mentorship back in the day as intangible and dominated by the "old boys' network." She continued, "The women who outranked me consistently said, 'I figured it all out by myself and you will too.'" In other words, no help at all. I promised myself that I would not be that woman, and I have not been. I try to teach, challenge, coach, and guide everyone with whom I work (men and women), and find it to be richly rewarding."

Fortunately, there is a more robust infrastructure to help aspiring female professionals, and many more people like my mom who try hard to help others.

But it's not enough.

The financial services industry where I spent my career is still plagued with too little diversity, particularly in leadership and executive roles. According to a March 2024 article in the American Bankers Association's ABA Banking Journal, "more than 50 percent of all U.S. bank employees are women, yet just 7.5 percent of banks are led by a woman CEO. The banking industry lags behind Fortune 500 companies, where 10.6 percent of all CEOs are women. While women earn more college degrees than men and rate higher on leadership competencies, just 32 percent of bank officers (vice presidents and higher) are women."

The root causes are big and small, and while some issues are larger than we can individually solve, there are things we can do. We can choose to mentor, sponsor and advocate for others as my mom did. We can hire based on strengths in lieu of experience whenever possible. We can continue to emphasize the importance of hiring for character, which will pay dividends in the future in recruiting. As Dutch Baughman, who appeared in Chapter 1, told me, "It's always been personal character. If you do an honest search as a leader, you can find people that have the skill sets in all the areas you need, but the determining factor has to be who has the strongest, genuine, authentic, personal character. You can go to war with that."

Strong, genuine, authentic, personal character. You have it or you don't. Those five traits from Chapter 4 that I'm so passionate about? Traits you look for to build your team around? None of those traits have anything to do with gender, color, age or religion. So don't carve out segments of the population when looking for them.

Poet Nikki Giovanni once famously said, "We are better than we think, and not quite what we want to be." It is true personally for all of us, to our own journeys, and in our quest to build organizations that represent the client bases we serve and the communities in which we work.

I'm proud of my mom and her journey, of what she has stood for and all she has become. And I made it my purpose, especially as my roles and influence got increasingly larger, to be a champion and advocate for women deserving of leadership positions.

In each of my last two career stops, I purposefully built leadership teams comprised predominantly of deserving women. In fact, in my last role at one point 100% of my leadership team and two-thirds of my people manager population was female. I tried very hard to bring to life the concepts in this book that I've written about in a way that aided in their development.

Also, in each of my last two stops, I intentionally recruited my eventual successor onto the leadership team within a year of starting with the company. Their names were Kelli Huber and Lisa Boylan, females I knew and respected and whose talents eclipsed mine in so many ways. I gave each of them support, stretch assignments, mentoring and a listening ear. Most importantly, I got out of their way and gave them a platform to shine.

I chose Kelli and Lisa as key right-hand leaders because they made our team stronger and they made me better. It was also an opportunity for each to prove that, when it was time for me to move on, they were a no-brainer to replace me.

This isn't reverse discrimination, not by a longshot. We always aim to hire the best candidate. I just happen to believe that in financial services, more often than acknowledged, the best candidate is, in fact, a woman.

We all pursue strategic business goals and organizational purpose to make a difference along the way. Weaving in personal purpose can be extremely rewarding, and allow you to have an impact far longer than you draw a paycheck.

This was my purpose.

Yours can be something else. What burns within you that might guide the way you lead others? Or pay it forward? The important thing is that you have one, and that it drives you.

I started this book with a story about how Steve Beck kicked off my self-awareness journey, and ended with a story about my mom and how it drove my purpose. Between those two formative experiences was a career-long collection of wins and losses, but more importantly, lessons.

Thirty years ago, I didn't have the tools necessary to build and lead organizations rooted in continuous improvement. I wasn't adept at leaving them better than I found them. I wasn't equipped to intentionally elevate women in leadership. I hadn't found my way yet. I hadn't learned what was important. I hadn't learned my craft. I hadn't learned to understand myself, much less those around me. I wasn't able to be the change I wanted to see in the world.

Gradually over time, I was.

Each of us moves through life, and our careers, capable of accomplishing so much and positively impacting the lives of others. It's through intentional effort, driven by purpose, that we learn to do so.

Here's to the journey.

Epilogue

Here's to the Journey

As I look back on the chapters of this book, I'm reminded that leadership isn't a destination. It's a practice. Leadership isn't defined by our job title or credentials; it's shaped by the way we prepare and show up in moments big and small. It's about how we treat people when no one's watching, how we stay steady as the stakes get higher, and how we stay committed to building something stronger, even when the path forward isn't clear.

Each chapter in this book reflects personal experiences and hard-earned lessons. I've shared stories of mentors, colleagues, and family members who've shaped my journey. I've reflected on wins and stumbles, moments of clarity and periods of growth.

In the introduction I lamented that, in contrast to how quickly we've advanced technologically, our collective leadership capabilities haven't seemed to keep pace. The reason, I believe, is two-fold. First, many companies fail to consistently prioritize helping people evolve and mature as leaders. Investing in human capital in this manner is often among the first to be cut when budgets tighten, so investments tend to happen in fits and starts, and they don't grow roots. This is both short-sighted and costly. Second, while I don't believe anyone *wants* to be a poor leader, not enough people prioritize improving as a leader and intentionally work towards that goal.

I've learned in life that, if something is important to you, you'll do it. For companies, I hope that they see the long-term value of developing leaders. For us individually, I hope we see the value in investing in ourselves.

Being a good leader and building a strong culture have got to be important to you if you want to lead others with any level of success.

And if there's a common thread through it all, it's this: we lead more effectively when we lead with purpose, and we find that purpose when we become more self-aware, more intentional, and more human. Thank you for joining me in this reflection. Whether you're a new or seasoned leader, I hope this book offered something valuable - a new perspective, a helpful reminder, or simply the encouragement to continue to work at being a better leader.

If you'd like to explore further, connect, or access additional tools and visual resources mentioned in the book (including full-color versions of the Cultural Themes, Anatomy of a Successful Team, and more), please visit www.paulpetera.com.

There, you'll find companion assets, leadership resources, and ways to engage with me, whether you're looking for thought partnership, mentoring, or merely a place to keep the conversation going.

Before we close, I want to share a few of my favorite quotes. These words have grounded me, challenged me, and reminded me why this work matters.

Here's to showing up with intention. To doing the enduring work.

Here's to leading, always, on purpose.

"Once you know who you are, you don't have to worry anymore."
— *Nikki Giovanni*

"People may forget what you said, they may forget what you did, but they will never forget how you made them feel."
— *Maya Angelou*

"A leader who is self-aware enough to know that he or she is not adept at everything is one who has taken the first step toward being a great leader."
— *Marshall Goldsmith*

"The X-factor of great leadership is not personality, it's humility."
— *Jim Collins*

"Personal leadership is the process of keeping your vision and values before you and aligning your life to be congruent with them."
— *Stephen Covey*

"If someone could only see my actions and not hear my words, what would they say are my priorities?"
— *James Clear*

"Greatness, it turns out, is largely a matter of conscious choice and discipline."
— *Jim Collins*

"The function of leadership isn't to produce more followers, it's to produce more leaders."
— *Ralph Nader*

"Gratitude kills pride. Gratitude removes selfishness. Gratitude slays self-sufficiency. Gratitude crushes the spirit of entitlement."
— *Unknown*

"Take care of your thoughts when you are alone. Take care of your words when you're with other people."
— *Unknown*

"Don't judge the journey before it's over. If you trust the promise, you have to trust the path. When you look for the good in everyone, you not only find it, you magnify it."
— *Steven Furtick*

Acknowledgments

We're born into this world with certain traits that shape who we are. Then we travel through life picking up, shedding, and gradually accumulating characteristics and behaviors based on our experiences that round out an ever-maturing version of who we are. This happens throughout the period of time between when we're born and when we die.

As a result of that journey, we grow, and that growth tends to showcase differences in our being through the years. In some ways, I'm the same kid I once was; in many others, I've grown into someone entirely different. Frankly, I am thankful for that, and there are so many people who had a hand in that growth and maturity.

I couldn't have gotten to this point in life without Andrea, my wife of over 30 years. Her support, patience and good-heartedness have been a rock without which I'd be lost and adrift. I certainly outkicked my coverage. Our daughter, Abby, has been our shining light since the day we brought her home, and is the reason why I worked so hard, sacrificed and tried to set a good example.

My parents, Anne and Ronnie, set great examples for me
in my formative years and beyond, and I couldn't have
asked for more. Andrea's mom, Linda, and her late father,
Tom, provided over 30 years of love and friendship that
I'll always be thankful for.

Believing in yourself is essential in life, but having others
believe in you is a gift worth appreciating. I'm thankful
that Steve Beck, Tarah Williams, David Kimm and Ron
Shandler believed in me at different points in my life.
Their decision to do so opened doors that allowed me to
grow as a professional and as a person.

There have been so many great leaders and thought
partners who have come into my life, and whose insights
spurred me to grow. Folks like Al Caiazzo, Joe Iraci,
Kevin Finn, Marv Adams, Elaine Logue, Paul Sternhagen,
Mitch Miles, Sue O'Donnell, Lisa Boylan, Kevin Gremer,
Marcus Johnson, Nick Drinkwine, Andy Deel, Shawn
Gilbert, Tom Macy, Dr. Kerry Smith, and Dutch
Baughman are just a few that I'm thankful for. There are
so many more.

Sports have always been important to me, and the art of
leadership in sports is as fascinating to watch as it is
applicable to our daily and work lives. I am thankful to
have had Frank Beamer represent my alma mater,
Virginia Tech, for so many years, and to lead in such a
thoughtful way, through good times and bad. Coach
Beamer was always fond of saying, "Take care of the little
things, and the big things will come" and "Never let the

highs get too high, or the lows get too low." Pretty good advice, and something I aspire to daily.

To the many teams and organizations that I've had the good fortune to lead - I appreciate your willingness to grow with me, share your knowledge and build together. I didn't always say or do the right thing, but every day, I tried to get 1% better. Even when, especially when, it was hard, I hope you know how much I cared for you, and how important it was to me to support you in your own journey.

Finally, I'm thankful for you, the reader. Being a good leader takes work. Building culture and helping others around you takes work. This world desperately needs more strong leaders. Each person who reads this book, shares it, and explores the resources referenced is helping prioritize and elevate leadership. It's through all of us and our intentional purpose-driven effort that we become better tomorrow than we were today.

Recommended Reading

The following books were referenced in, or influenced, *Built on Purpose* to support key leadership ideas and offer further depth for readers interested in exploring these topics more fully.

Collins, Jim. *Good to Great: Why Some Companies Make the Leap… and Others Don't.* HarperBusiness, 2001.
→ Referenced for ideas on humility, disciplined leadership, and long-term impact.

Covey, Stephen R. *Principle-Centered Leadership.* Free Press, 1991.
→ Referenced for the importance of values, alignment, and self-management in effective leadership.

Edmondson, Amy C. *The Fearless Organization: Creating Psychological Safety in the Workplace for Learning, Innovation, and Growth.* Wiley, 2018.
→ Referenced for ideas on psychological safety and supporting team performance through trust.

Eurich, Tasha. *Insight: Why We're Not as Self-Aware as We Think, and How Seeing Ourselves Clearly Helps Us Succeed at Work and in Life.* Crown Business, 2017.
→ Referenced for research on self-awareness, reflection, and feedback techniques.

George, Bill. *True North: Discover Your Authentic Leadership.* Jossey-Bass, 2007.
→ Referenced for insights on authentic leadership and values-based decision-making.

Gladwell, Malcolm. *Blink: The Power of Thinking Without Thinking.* Little, Brown and Company, 2005.
→ Referenced for thoughts on first impressions and intuitive judgment.

Gladwell, Malcolm. *Outliers: The Story of Success.* Little, Brown and Company, 2008.
→ Referenced for the role of practice and mastery in leadership.

Goleman, Daniel. *Emotional Intelligence: Why It Can Matter More Than IQ.* Bantam, 1995.
→ Referenced for the four EQ domains and the foundation of emotional intelligence in leadership.

Kline, Nancy. *Time to Think: Listening to Ignite the Human Mind.* Cassell Illustrated, 1999.
→ Referenced for creating environments that foster deeper thinking and reflection.

Kotter, John P. *Leading Change.* Harvard Business Review Press, 1996.
→ Referenced for change management models and building organizational momentum.

Lencioni, Patrick. *The Advantage: Why Organizational Health Trumps Everything Else in Business.* Jossey-Bass, 2012.
→ Referenced for the importance of clarity, trust, and culture as cornerstones of effective leadership.

Maxwell, John C. *The 21 Irrefutable Laws of Leadership.* Thomas Nelson, 2007.

→ Referenced for reflections on leadership influence, trust, and growth.

McKeown, Greg. *Essentialism: The Disciplined Pursuit of Less.* Crown Business, 2014.
→ Referenced for the concept of boundaries, prioritization, and strategic focus.

Powell, Colin. *It Worked for Me: In Life and Leadership.* Harper, 2012.
→ Referenced for insights into intentional communication and leadership presence.

Watkins, Michael D. *The First 90 Days: Proven Strategies for Getting Up to Speed Faster and Smarter.* Harvard Business Review Press, 2013.
→ Referenced for the STaRS framework and situational leadership alignment.

Wiseman, Liz. *Multipliers: How the Best Leaders Make Everyone Smarter.* HarperBusiness, 2010.
→ Referenced for insights on leadership that expands the intelligence and capability of teams.

If *Built on Purpose* resonated with you, I'd be incredibly grateful if you shared your thoughts in a review. Your feedback helps more readers discover the book, and helps me continue to grow and improve as a writer and leader.

Leave a review and spread the word.
Thank you for being part of the journey.

Amazon:

PETERA

LEADERSHIP GROUP

www.ingramcontent.com/pod-product-compliance
Lightning Source LLC
Chambersburg PA
CBHW020159090426
42734CB00008B/879